Praise for *The Leader's Guide to Presenting*

'An indispensable guide for global leaders in aiding the preparation of high-stakes, persuasive presentations with structure and purpose to deliver positive outcomes. This book has been an invaluable aid in delivering to my audiences engaging and compelling messages with the necessary punch!! Brilliant!!'

**Dr Graham Woolford, Head of Operations,
Unihealth, South Africa**

'Having coached and trained leaders since 1999, including presentations coaching and training, I am hugely impressed with Jeremy and Tom's book. *The Leader's Guide to Presenting* provides leaders with a thorough, practical and easy to use guide to making presentations to different types of audience. I've learned a lot from reading it.'

**Jeremy Lazarus MA, FCCA, FCT, Director,
The Lazarus Consultancy Ltd**

'This book crystallises the key elements that can allow any leader to be really present when they present and make a dynamic difference with any audience. You can dip into it or read it in a linear way – whichever way you chose I can guarantee you will find lots of ideas, tools and questions that will allow you to improve your ability to present dynamically and make the impact that will make a real, positive difference in your world.'

John Matson, Partner, Arthur Cox, Chair, Lex Mundi

'When you present, who you are is on display just as much as the material you are presenting. Tom and Jeremy have nailed this with simple and practical exercises to help any presenter discover more about how they show up to an audience. Critical presentations, perhaps more than any others, require the presenter to win the hearts of the audience before it becomes possible to move them with information and win their minds. This is a great step-by-step guide to doing so. I found myself thinking, "I hope the next presenter I see has read this book".'

Paul Matthews, founder and MD, People Alchemy

'An essential and practical resource for any leader who wants to ensure their presentations drive real impact.'

Penny Shaw, Chief Risk Officer, Chaucer plc

'This is the most effective book I have ever read on the art of presenting, especially for leaders. It truly covers every aspect of presenting effectively to achieve change and motivation within your own organisation or to other groups. It is compelling, interesting and ground breaking in its method and approach. I have already applied the material here to excellent effect and would highly recommend *The Leader's Guide to Presenting* for any aspiring leaders and presenters as the one book they would ever need on this subject. I think it will become a standard work in the years to come.'

Adrian Foster, UK Marketing Manager, Parker Hannifin

'I coach many executives how to present. Once they read this book, they will find it impossible to give a bad presentation. Too many senior people struggle with too many elements of presenting, even though they understand how important it is nowadays in winning hearts and minds. I have seen Tom and Jeremy deliver highly impressive training and now they have created a book that forensically examines every aspect of this vital area of leadership. It's the right book at the right time. It is bold, yet sensible, profound, yet practical, and it is applicable to many different situations where you need to improve the way you communicate and influence.'

Neil Mullarkey, the UK's leading improviser and experienced leadership trainer and coach

'Tom and Jeremy have worked very effectively with many leaders in our firm both in the UK and internationally. We all know the old line about failing to prepare and preparing to fail, BUT this book gives you real insights into how to do that. The versatility and skills of the authors come through with this complete package: showing you how to bring out your own personal style as well as how to make the most impact. It will help you become a more complete and engaging presenter. I'll be using it in my role!'

Paul Rawlinson, Global Chairman, Baker & McKenzie

The Leader's Guide to Presenting

Pearson

At Pearson, we believe in learning – all kinds of learning for all kinds of people. Whether it's at home, in the classroom or in the workplace, learning is the key to improving our life chances.

That's why we're working with leading authors to bring you the latest thinking and best practices, so you can get better at the things that are important to you. You can learn on the page or on the move, and with content that's always crafted to help you understand quickly and apply what you've learned.

If you want to upgrade your personal skills or accelerate your career, become a more effective leader or more powerful communicator, discover new opportunities or simply find more inspiration, we can help you make progress in your work and life.

Every day our work helps learning flourish, and wherever learning flourishes, so do people.

To learn more, please visit us at **www.pearson.com/uk**

The Financial Times

With a worldwide network of highly respected journalists, *The Financial Times* provides global business news, insightful opinion and expert analysis of business, finance and politics. With over 500 journalists reporting from 50 countries worldwide, our in-depth coverage of international news is objectively reported and analysed from an independent, global perspective.

To find out more, visit **www.ft.com**

The Leader's Guide to Presenting

How to use soft skills
to get hard results

Tom Bird and Jeremy Cassell

 Pearson

Harlow, England • London • New York • Boston • San Francisco • Toronto • Sydney
Dubai • Singapore • Hong Kong • Tokyo • Seoul • Taipei • New Delhi
Cape Town • São Paulo • Mexico City • Madrid • Amsterdam • Munich • Paris • Milan

PEARSON EDUCATION LIMITED

Edinburgh Gate
Harlow CM20 2JE
United Kingdom
Tel: +44 (0)1279 623623
Web: www.pearson.com/uk

First edition published 2017 (print and electronic)
© Pearson Education Limited 2017 (print and electronic)

The rights of Tom Bird and Jeremy Cassell to be identified as authors of this work have been asserted by them in accordance with the Copyright, Designs and Patents Act 1988.

ISBN: 978–1-292–11998–4 (print)
      978–1-292–11999–1 (PDF)
      978–1-292–12001–0 (ePub)

British Library Cataloguing-in-Publication Data
A catalogue record for the print edition is available from the British Library

Library of Congress Cataloging-in-Publication Data

Names: Bird, Tom, 1964– author. | Cassell, Jeremy, author.
Title: The leader's guide to presenting : how to use soft skills to get hard results / Tom Bird and Jeremy Cassell.
Description: 1 Edition. | New York: Pearson Education, 2017. | Series: The leader's guide | Includes index.
Identifiers: LCCN 2016051280 (print) | LCCN 2016054049 (ebook) | ISBN 9781292119984 (pbk.) | ISBN 9781292119991 (PDF) | ISBN 9781292120010 (ePub) | ISBN 9781292120010
Subjects: LCSH: Business presentations.
Classification: LCC HF5718.22 .B57 2017 (print) | LCC HF5718.22 (ebook) | DDC 658.4/52—dc23
LC record available at https://lccn.loc.gov/2016051280

10 9 8 7 6 5 4 3 2 1
21 20 19 18 17

Print edition typeset in 9/13 Melior Com Regular by iEnergizer Aptara®, Ltd.
Printed by Ashford Colour Press Ltd., Gosport

NOTE THAT ANY PAGE CROSS REFERENCES REFER TO THE PRINT EDITION

Contents

part 6 Your path to presenting success

About the authors

Tom Bird is a trainer, speaker and coach specialising in high-stakes presentation skills, influencing, sales and business development. Since 2001, after a 12-year career running software businesses, Tom has worked with a wide range of FTSE and professional service firms (he is a founding partner of the Møller PSF Group – www.mollercentre.co.uk/psfg/) worldwide to help improve the performance of their senior people. He is a Master Practitioner of NLP, holds business and finance qualifications from Kingston Business School and has a Postgraduate Diploma in Coaching and Development from the University of Portsmouth. Tom can be contacted for training and coaching work at tom@rtpc.co.uk

Jeremy Cassell is a trainer, coach and keynote speaker, working with a wide range of international companies and professional services firms. After graduating with an English degree, he worked as a teacher, a salesman and the training manager for L'Oreal and Pepsi before starting RTP (www.rtpc.co.uk) in 2000. He is a partner at The Moller Group (www.mollercentre.co.uk/psfg) and works with senior business people focusing on improving their influencing, selling and presentation skills. He can be contacted via email for one-to-one coaching or group work on improving presentation skills at jeremy@rtpc.co.uk.

Together, Jeremy and Tom are co-authors of four business books including *The FT Guide to Business Training* and the bestselling *Brilliant Selling*.

Acknowledgements

We are grateful to the following for permission to reproduce copyright material:

Figure on p. 10 reproduced courtesy of Des Woods, Partner, Møller PSF Group, Cambridge; figure on p. 102 reprinted with the permission of Scribner, a division of Simon & Schuster, Inc. from *On Death and Dying* by Dr Elisabeth Kübler-Ross. Copyright © 1969 by Elisabeth Kübler-Ross; copyright renewed © 1997 by Elisabeth Kübler-Ross. All rights reserved.

Introduction

S o much of your success in business hangs on your ability to present effectively in high-stakes situations.

Whatever your functional role, as a leader there will be times when it is critical for you to be able to engage, motivate, inform or gain commitment from a group through some form of presentation. In these situations, the outcome of your presentation has fundamental importance in taking you towards achieving your business goals. These are high-stakes situations.

This book

There are hundreds of books on presentation skills available and you chose this one. This is the right choice for you if you are looking for an all-encompassing, comprehensive guide to designing, delivering and following up on high-stakes presentations. It is also the right book for you if you present as a leader because there are often specific considerations to take account of when you are presenting and have a leadership position. Finally, it is also the right book if you are looking for practical tips and tools that you can apply to improve every presentation you deliver.

We have written this book because we work with people like you every day, supporting them and helping them with their high-stakes presentations. We train groups in how to present effectively and we coach senior business leaders in their specific high-stakes presentations. We provide this support internationally, working extensively in Europe, the Middle East, Asia and the United States. In this work, with both individual leaders and with groups, we see some common issues when it comes to presenting and we know how to address them. This is a very practical 'how to' book based on our work with thousands of people over the last 16 years, our research into highly effective presenters and the research of others that has contributed to what we believe works.

You are likely to be someone who fits into one or more of the following categories:

▌ a manager in a business in which you have responsibility for a team of people and need to achieve certain specific Key Performance Indicators or business outcomes;

▌ a departmental leader who needs to work with other leaders and departments as well as the people you manage;

▌ a board member with executive responsibility, possibly in a large corporate business;

▌ an entrepreneur who needs to engage and influence a wide variety of stakeholders;

▌ someone who recognises the importance of delivering effective presentations as a way of influencing others.

What is a presentation and what makes it 'high-stakes'?

For a book that focuses on presenting we should at the very least give you our working definition of what a presentation is and what constitutes a 'high-stakes' presentation as this sets the tone for everything we cover in *The Leader's Guide to Presenting*.

For us, a presentation is any time, formally or informally, when the spotlight is on you to deliver information to a group with the express intention to inform, galvanise to action, engage, motivate or persuade.

A high-stakes presentation is one in which securing a positive outcome is critical (rather than just desirable) to you. They may not happen every day or indeed every month but when these presentation opportunities do occur there is a lot riding on the outcome for you.

Examples include:

▌ conference presentations in which your credibility and brand may be at stake;

▌ board presentations in which you might be seeking support for a proposal and where your personal reputation might be impacted if you deliver poorly;

▌ pitching for a significant contract or piece of work, either on your own or as part of a senior pitch team;

▌ securing commitment and buy-in from your team around a proposed change;

▌ seeking funding or approval for something that is of strategic importance;

▌ presenting an annual business plan to your team and wanting to engage their support and commitment to it.

And you will be able to come up with many more examples that are relevant to you.

What is our approach and what does this book cover?

It would be easy to write a relatively short book that simply equips you with all of the 'best practice' around how you should go about designing and delivering an effective presentation. Our belief is that presenting as a leader in high-stakes situations requires much more than that if you are to be really effective. While design and delivery are important, there are other aspects that need to be considered if you are to be seen as being authentic as well as effective when you present.

The following four-layer model for effective high-stakes presenting details our approach and philosophy:

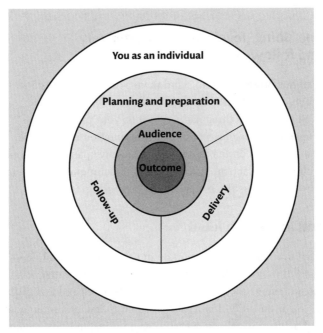

The four-layer model for effective high-stakes presenting

Outcome

At the centre of our model is your outcome. All high-stakes presentations need to be built around a desired outcome; it is the reason that you are presenting and needs to be the start point of the process. This book will help you consider your outcomes and ensure they are realistic.

Audience

You are seeking to achieve an outcome with or through your audience. Their context, reality and feelings will all impact your ability to achieve the outcome and so you need to consider them carefully. This book is written specifically to help you take account of what your audience needs from you in order to maximise the chance of achieving your desired outcome.

The 'doing' level – planning, delivery and follow-up

For your presentation to stand the maximum chance of achieving the desired outcome with your audience you need to focus on three main elements: your planning and preparation, the delivery of your presentation itself, and how you follow up on the presentation. We have packed the book with lots of practical 'how to' tips and techniques that focus on each of these three elements of presenting.

You as an individual

Surrounding everything you do in your planning, delivery and follow-up and, indeed, how you view your outcome and the audience, are the beliefs, skills, awareness and flexibility of you as an individual. Your personal character, preferences and habits will inform everything you think and do so a large part of this book asks you to develop increased awareness of these aspects.

This book and your presentations

We have focused on creating a practical book that can be a real resource wherever you are in your journey as a presenter and wherever you are in thinking about specific presentations. While you can read this book from 'cover to cover' it is equally appropriate to dip into it to get whatever you need 'in the moment'. We have structured the book so that it is split into logical sections, so whether you are at the early stages of planning a high-stakes presentation or whether you need some quick design or delivery tips, you will be able to find what you want.

But it does not stop there. We have created a website packed with additional 'just-in-time' resources and ideas that you can have free access to. These will support you in improving the structure, impact and delivery of every presentation you make. Just register at www.theleadersguidetopresenting.com. You can use the site to give you further inspiration for your presentations and make contact with us should you be looking for more individual support around creating and delivering impactful, high-stakes presentations.

Above all, remember that becoming outstanding as a presenter is a contact sport: it is only by looking for more opportunities to present and gaining more experience in presenting that you will improve and develop. Our intention is to equip you with all of the ideas, techniques and approaches that some of the best and most experienced presenters wish they had learned sooner.

Enjoy the book and start utilising the key take-aways in your own high-stakes presentations.

Part 1

Who are you as a presenter?

Who are you when you present?

Great leaders understand themselves well. They think carefully about the impact they have on others.

▌ How much of you as a person do your people see when you present?

▌ To what extent do you focus on the impact you will make as a leader when you present?

If this were simply a book to teach presentation skills we would dive right into techniques, structures and practical tips to improve your effectiveness. But this book is about delivering powerful presentations with impact and influence, as a leader. To do this, you have to recognise the particular considerations that come with your leadership role.

It may be that your particular specialist knowledge has served you well in getting into a leadership position but it is unlikely to be enough to ensure you are seen as an effective leader, particularly in the context of presenting. Often, your specific area of expertise is where you are most comfortable: being able to add value through your subject-matter knowledge. Knowledge is of course a key pillar in your ability to lead and yet when you present it will only be one of a number of factors that will allow you to influence effectively.

> Knowledge ... will only be one of a number of factors that will allow you to influence effectively.

Consider these two quotations:

> 'Leadership is the art of getting someone else to do something you want done because he wants to do it.'
> Dwight D. Eisenhower

> 'If your actions inspire others to dream more, learn more, do more and become more, you are a leader.' John Quincy Adams

Neither of these quotes focus on knowledge. Instead they speak to your ability to engage and influence.

How you are seen and perceived by others is critical to achieving engagement and influence and so before you consider the 'how to' of presenting effectively it is important to think about 'who you are': both what you stand for as a leader and how you are perceived by those you are and will be presenting to.

You'll know the phrase 'perception is reality' and this is particularly true when you are in a leadership position. As a leader, you are seen and experienced by others for more than just your specialist knowledge. For example, recent research shows that many Venture Capitalists are assessing *how* someone presents a proposition to them and are asking the question 'Are *they* buying what they're selling?' People will be making judgements about you when you present. As human beings we typically interpret and make meaning of what we see – we rarely see things objectively. Instead, we delete, distort and generalise our experience in order to make meaning of it.

This concept is easily explained by the Fundamental Attribution Error: a process we all go through many times a day when we interact with others.

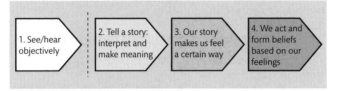

The Fundamental Attribution Error

Whenever we see someone present we are (1) observing specific behaviours and hearing their words objectively. But human beings are meaning-making creatures and so, in the absence of knowing their feelings, beliefs and motivations we (2) infer these from what we see and hear and how it is presented. At this point we are 'telling ourselves a story' and are no longer making meaning based on purely objective fact. We have crossed a line from thinking objectively to thinking subjectively. This inference leads us to (3) feel a certain way, and this feeling is what creates our perceptions and beliefs about the other person. Importantly, we act on our beliefs and on how we feel about a person, their proposition and how their presentation makes us feel.

Your audience is experiencing this unconscious process every time they see you present.

Authenticity

A critical part of the answer to the question 'Who are you when you present?' lies in the need for you to be authentic. It is important for you to be seen very much as yourself when you present, rather than as an actor playing a role. Authenticity is about being genuine. Studies show that the harder interviewees work to manage the impression they make, the more they seem insincere. By focusing on the impression you make on yourself instead of others you can be more authentic when you present. Good advice for presenters is to focus on being a bigger version of yourself when you are presenting.

> Focus on being a bigger version of yourself when you are presenting.

Some questions will help raise awareness about 'who you are when you present':

▌ What's important to you about being a leader?

▌ What's important to you about your people?

▌ How would your people describe you as a leader?

▌ How would they describe you as a presenter?

▌ How would you *like* them to describe you?

▌ What are your specific strengths as a leader?

▌ What are the areas you know you need to work on?

▌ When you present, how much emotion do you display?

▌ How much of you as a person do your people see when you present?

▌ Do you feel confident when you present? Do you have the same confidence level in all presentation situations? If not, when is your confidence higher than normal? When is it lower than normal?

What does being authentic mean in practice? The word originates from the Greek word 'authentikos' meaning genuine. You need to both *be* genuine and *appear* genuine when you present. This requires you to be very clear on what you stand for, but it also requires you to be aware of how you are seen by others so that you can proactively manage their perception of you. This proactive management of their perception is not at odds with being authentic. If you are clear on what you stand for and on what you believe in, then it is entirely appropriate to maximise the chances of being successful through managing how you present to increase your effectiveness. Being authentic is a state that you can manage rather than a trait that is genetically determined.

If you are authentic, you are seen by others as demonstrating and delivering on the things that are important to you through how you communicate and present. If you feel passionate about something when you present, then this passion is visible to your audience. If you are confident of achieving an outcome, this confidence comes across both in your words and, more importantly, through your tone of voice and body language. In short, the message conveyed in your words is congruent with how you convey those words.

The question of authenticity introduces three specific questions the leader should usefully consider:

1. Does the way I present as a leader communicate the things that I feel and want others to feel?

2. What do I need to do if it does not?

3. What do I do when I need to engage a group around something that I may not be engaged about myself?

While this book will provide a lot of practical guidance and techniques to ensure that your presentations are impactful and influential, the specific challenges of presenting as a leader can only be fully met if you have two things in spades:

- self-awareness; and
- behavioural flexibility.

No behaviour change can occur without first having self-awareness. In this context, you need to have awareness about what you stand for as a leader, how you are seen and experienced by others when you present, how you deliver messages when you are passionate and believe in them and how you come across when you do not have as much passion or belief in the message you are conveying.

> No behaviour change can occur without first having self-awareness.

Once you have self-awareness you can focus on developing and demonstrating behavioural flexibility. This concept was well known to Einstein who said: 'The definition of madness is consistently doing the same thing and expecting a different result.' Put more simply, if what you are doing is not working, do something different. This is particularly important if you want to change how you present in certain circumstances: you need to have the flexibility to try a different approach which, at first, might not feel as comfortable as how you have presented in the past.

What does my audience need from me when I present?

When you present as a leader, it is helpful to think about what *type* of leadership your audience might need when you are presenting and how this differs from your daily leadership activities. The leadership that is needed when you are working with individuals in the office is very different from that required during high-stakes presentations and so you need to adapt your style and approach to meet the needs of the situation. Des Woods, a partner at The Møller PSF Group, Cambridge and a leadership expert, has identified three different 'states' of leadership that are helpful to consider.

'Sitting down' leadership

When you are working with your people on a daily basis to get the work done, your leadership is focused on situations where there is often clarity around the outcomes and the methods needed to achieve those outcomes. In these situations, your people benefit from what we might call 'sitting down' leadership. This type of leadership is about offering feedback and guidance, often through taking a coaching approach.

'Standing up' leadership

When either the desired outcomes or the methods to achieve them are unclear to your people they require more visible and visionary leadership. We might call this 'standing up' leadership in that they need to see you. You are likely to be communicating a message to the group rather than to individuals and you need to bring clarity.

'Standing on a chair' leadership

When both desired outcomes and methods lack clarity – often in times of change, for example, when a lot of things are ambiguous and fluid – your people need stronger and very visible leadership. They might need to feel inspired and confident in you, and be convinced by your message, which, in turn, requires you to be seen to be calm and confident when giving direction.

The diagram below illustrates this model and looks at the clarity (or lack of) around the goals and methods for achieving those goals, as ways of helping to determine what type of leadership is needed by your people.

When you present as a leader you are likely to be engaged in either 'standing up' or 'standing on a chair' leadership and being effective in these situations requires you to know how your messaging needs to be adapted compared to your everyday leadership situations in order to be effective. We look at how to do this in Chapters 2 and 3.

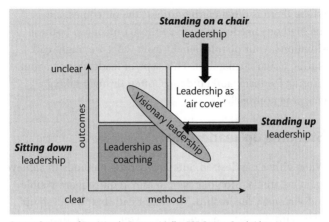

Source: Courtesy of Des Woods, Partner, Møller PSF Group, Cambridge.

Example

James managed his department competently and quietly. His people saw him as a 'safe pair of hands' and appreciated his calm manner and the regular feedback he gave that helped individuals make 'small adjustments to the tiller' to ensure that objectives were met. His 'sitting down' leadership was faultless.

But change was afoot. The leadership team required him to implement a new system that would change how his people worked and require them to interact more closely with other departments. There would be a period of adjustment during which the processes and ways of working would need to flex. James had thought about this and was behind the change – he could see the benefits but he knew that some of his team would struggle as they were not exposed to the wider business realities that he was. While he was engaged and committed, he worried that his team would resist and resent the change.

What was needed was 'standing on a chair' leadership. James needed to connect with his beliefs around the change, its benefits and the reasons behind it. Rather than provide a purely factual presentation on what would happen, he needed to articulate clearly the reasons behind the change, show his team that he was committed to it, that he recognised the challenges but had his eye on the longer-term picture. His team needed to see and feel this from his presentation and it needed to be genuine in order to be believed. The words would take second place to the perception he created. James created a presentation that articulated a compelling reason for the change. He used examples of specific tasks that would be easier after the change and looked outside of his business for other industry examples that underpinned the benefits that could be gained from the change. He demonstrated empathy for the fact that it would not be easy but confirmed his commitment to supporting his people and achieving success. He finished by articulating the first key steps and his expectations of his team. All of his team received a compelling, consistent and passionate message backed up by a clear call to action. This was 'standing on a chair' leadership.

SUMMARY

▌ As a leader, your presentations are often more than just about facts and information – you need to engage, motivate and influence.

▌ People make judgements about *you* when you present – focus on how you want to be perceived by others rather than just on the content alone.

▌ Being authentic when you present as a leader is critical: the audience must see you as genuine.

▌ Self-awareness and behavioural flexibility are critical to maximising your impact and influence when you present.

▌ Presentations by a leader are often high-stakes, 'standing on a chair' leadership. This requires you to be a bigger version of yourself, to provide visible, strong leadership.

How do people perceive and experience you when you present?

Think about some leaders' presentations that you have attended in the past – the good and the bad. What do you recall about them? Do you recall specific messages, words and content or do you recall perceptions you had about the person or the feelings you experienced while they presented?

For most people it is a combination of both but, importantly, being on the receiving end of a presentation often gives rise to feelings in you. They might be feelings of confidence in the presenter, belief in their passion and trust in their ability. Alternatively, they might be feelings around a lack of confidence or commitment, uncertainty or distrust. The Fundamental Attribution Error discussed in Chapter 1 will play a part in creating these feelings.

The question of how people perceive and experience us when we present is an important one. It has little to do with the structure that we have created for the presentation or even the words that we have spent time planning. Perception arises from unconscious judgements that we make from the moment someone starts to present, and so these judgements spring from our body language and voice.

Before we can manage these perceptions of us by others we need to first understand what they are. Outstanding presenters manage the perceptions others have of them by first understanding how they are experienced by others and then applying behavioural flexibility to manage or alter these perceptions.

Raising your own awareness about the impact you have when presenting

When you present, does your audience see you as a calm, confident leader who is clear about your goal and in your thinking about how to achieve it? Do they experience any stress when you are presenting or uncertainty in either the content or the reasoning you are communicating? Do they connect and engage with your message because you are communicating in a way that works for them? In short, what is the feeling that you, as a leader, leave them with at the end of your presentation?

Taking the time to reflect on how you come across to others is important and some useful questions that you can easily consider include:

▌ Being objective and putting myself in the audience's shoes, how might I be being perceived when I present right now?

▌ How do I want people to perceive me when I present?

▌ What do I stand for as a leader and how can I communicate this through my presentations?

The following exercise might be helpful in gaining a greater degree of awareness and some insight into where you might focus your behavioural flexibility.

Awareness: taking different perspectives

This exercise encourages you to take different perspectives on the same event and can help you learn more about how you came across and give you ideas about what to do differently to manage the perception others have of you in similar situations. To be most effective, you need to fully engage with each position, thinking as if you are in that position.

First position

Recall a time when you gave a presentation where, as you look back on it now, you would have liked to have made more impact or achieved a different outcome. Take a few minutes to really recall the event. Remember the people who were in the audience, how you were feeling at the time, what your key messages were and how the presentation went.

From this perspective, answer the following questions:

▌ How am I feeling just before I start the presentation?

▌ What are the thoughts that are going through my mind?

▌ What are my hopes and fears for this presentation?

▌ What do I need my audience to think and feel at the end of it?

▌ How might they be feeling about the presentation topic before I start?

Second position

Now imagine you are a member of the audience for the presentation. It often helps to physically move into a different space or chair to further encourage you to think from this new perspective. Thinking now as a member of the audience, consider the following questions:

▌ How are you feeling at the start of the presentation?

▌How do you feel about the topic that is to be presented?

▌What do you need from the presenter to maximise the impact and value of this presentation?

▌How do you think the presenter looks as they prepare to present?

▌How do you think the presenter is feeling about the topic and the audience as they get ready to present?

▌What individual descriptive words come to mind about the presenter as they are presenting?

▌What advice would you give the presenter to help create the feeling that you want in order to gain most value from the presentation?

Third position

Finally, imagine that you are an impartial external observer looking in on the presentation and seeing both the presenter and the audience. You might again benefit from moving physically to help take on this different perspective on the presentation. Thinking now as this impartial observer, consider the following questions:

▌What do you notice about the atmosphere in the room during the presentation?

▌What do you notice about the audience and how they are reacting?

▌What do you notice about the presenter?

▌What specific advice would you give the presenter to maximise the positive impact and influence they have?

This awareness-raising exercise can be used to think about presentations you have given in the past but can also be a useful part of your planning for a future presentation.

Observe yourself

When we teach presentation skills to leaders we try to use video whenever possible. Why? Because seeing yourself on video and hearing how your voice sounds to an audience is a great way of raising awareness and creating immediate positive behaviour change. While it is the element in any training that is least looked forward to by participants, we often find that it gains the most positive feedback after the event.

Ask someone to video a presentation that you give or arrange it yourself with a smartphone. Watching this back and making notes about what you notice can quickly improve how you come across when you present.

> Seeing yourself on video and hearing how your voice sounds to an audience is a great way of raising awareness and creating immediate positive behaviour change.

Seek feedback

Your own views on how you are perceived by others are helpful in raising awareness but seeking other people's views can bring about a step change in your presenting. Given the significant value of seeking and receiving feedback on how you are perceived by others when you are presenting, it is somewhat surprising how rarely it is done.

Often, what stops us seeking feedback is linked with one or more of the following:

▌ We are fearful of what people might say.

▌ We think that they will say only positive things to avoid hurting our feelings.

▐ Their feedback will be too generic to add much value (for example, 'you were really good').

▐ We don't think to ask for feedback.

▐ We are unsure about who to ask and what they might think of the request.

There may be other interferences that you can think of but, if you look at the list, we have some element of control over all of them. The secret to asking for feedback and maximising the value of it is in *how* you ask.

> The secret to asking for feedback and maximising the value of it is in *how* you ask.

Here are some practical tips around seeking feedback from others.

1. **Articulate *why* you are seeking feedback.** Helping others understand your reason for seeking feedback from them gives them the context for feedback. If they know why you are seeking feedback they are better able to give relevant and useful feedback.

2. **Be specific.** Tell them what, specifically, you would like feedback on as this will focus their attention on the things that are important to you. This might be around engaging the audience, how confident or believable you came across, how you handled questions, the quality of your content or the structure of the presentation, for example.

3. **Focus on objectivity and give examples.** Feedback is most useful when it is objective so encourage people to give feedback on specific behaviours, approaches, body language and words that they observe or hear. Give examples of how you would like the feedback so they are clear on what is useful to you. For example, you might

ask: 'I would like feedback on the extent to which I come across as either possessing or lacking confidence. Can you make a note of the specific things you see or hear that contribute to your view of my confidence level and when in the presentation I demonstrated them.' Remember that a face-to-face communication comprises the words, how you say the words (voice and tone) and physiology (body language). Seek feedback that focuses on each of these specific areas.

4. **Think about who to ask.** It might be easy to ask people who know you well for feedback but it might be more relevant and helpful to seek feedback from others who know you less well. Think about the audiences you present to and who might be representative of that community that could give you valuable feedback. Try to seek feedback from a few people, ideally in different positions in the business, so you can notice trends in what you hear.

5. **Hear the feedback immediately after the presentation if possible.** Your presentation will be fresh in the other person's mind – not just what they saw and heard but how they felt as a result.

Your reaction to feedback

It is one thing to seek feedback from others, but what if we don't like what we hear? The benefit of feedback is that it makes us consciously aware of things that we might be doing that either support and contribute to our effectiveness or get in the way of it when we present. In a very real way, therefore, feedback is a gift. As with any gift, we can make the choice to either accept it or reject it.

If feedback is given based on observed behaviours then it is likely to be more objective than subjective. It is important that we hear objective feedback and consider it. Often, how we feel about feedback (particularly feedback that appears negative to us) changes after we have slept on it. After a little time we can revisit the feedback we received and choose whether to act on it, seek further clarification from the giver or reject it. By seeking feedback from different people we can pay attention to any trends in the feedback that we receive.

SUMMARY

▍ Outstanding presenters manage the perceptions others have of them by first understanding how they are experienced by others and then applying behavioural flexibility to manage or alter these perceptions.

▍ Reflecting on past presentations from three different perspectives – you as the presenter, the audience and an independent observer – raises awareness about how you may be perceived.

▍ Seeking feedback identifies the perceptions others have of you.

▍ Tell people why you want feedback and the specific areas of your presentation that you are looking for feedback on.

▍ Ask and probe for objective feedback: what they notice about your words, voice and body language and what is the impact it has on them?

▍ Genuinely listen to and consider their feedback: does it fit with the feedback you have received from others? Make a considered choice to accept, seek clarification on or reject each piece of feedback.

3 Managing perception

We have discussed how, as a leader, your presentations create certain perceptions in the mind of the audience and that these perceptions are based on largely unconscious judgements. This is important because people buy into ideas emotionally first and then justify them logically. Once you have identified how people perceive you when you present you can turn your attention to managing these perceptions.

> People buy into ideas emotionally first and then justify them logically.

Managing the perceptions of others is something that you can do consciously and proactively; it is a matter of influencing. While you cannot control how others perceive you and think about you, you can influence them through demonstrating awareness and behavioural flexibility.

What are some practical steps that you can take to manage the perceptions of others?

Know specifically how you want to be perceived

Managing perception must start with clarity around how you want to be perceived. We have posed some questions to help this thinking process in Chapter 2 but it is worth getting very clear and specific if you are to maximise your chance of achieving success. Studies by Amy Cuddy show that people ask and answer the following two questions when they meet someone new:

▌ Can I trust this person?

▌ Can I respect this person?

While trust and respect might be quite universal in terms of aspects of the perception you want to communicate, there may be other aspects that are also important.

Although some presentations might require you to communicate certain very specific traits and emotions, it is likely that as a leader there will be a core set of values, traits and emotions that represent who you are and how you would like to be seen by others.

Complete this exercise:

Exercise

1. **What specific words describe how you would like others to perceive you?** For the purposes of this book the context is around how you want to be perceived when you present. These words will be personal to you and will depend on your values, beliefs, environment and culture (both personal and organisational). They might also be informed by any feedback you have received on how you come across.

Some examples of words that might emerge include: calm, trustworthy, credible, confident, committed, passionate, motivated, inspiring, understanding.

▶

2. **Do these traits feel authentic to you?** As you look at the list of words you came up with, do any of them jar with your beliefs about yourself, what you stand for or who you are? Do some resonate more than others? For any that jar with you, what is it about them that causes concern and are there any specific contexts where the traits would resonate more? Is it that they don't feel authentic to you or is it that you don't see yourself as communicating the traits right now when you present?

It is sometimes easy to dismiss a trait that we would like to see ourselves communicating when we present simply because we do not know *how* to communicate it. Being clear on whether it is an identity or skill issue will help.

3. **What are my priorities?** As you look at the list, what are the most important traits that you want to communicate? Relative to how you present now, where, in your opinion, are the biggest gaps? Focus on two or three traits that you feel will have maximum impact if you were able to communicate them more effectively when you present.

4. **What, specifically, would demonstrate these important traits?** Once you have established your priorities, you can work on developing how you communicate them. Improving how you present is rarely down to focusing on one thing in isolation; it is about planning, structure, content, managing your state and delivery techniques. Simply putting your awareness on your key priorities for managing others' perceptions of you will help focus your mind on what you can do differently. The remainder of this chapter and the rest of this book will equip you with more ideas, tools and techniques.

Look at role models for the characteristics you want to communicate

Think back to some of the most useful things you have learned in the past. These might include learning to walk, learning to talk or learning how to interact as part of a group situation. All of these are examples of skills that you started to develop through observational learning. Observational learning is based on a learner first observing then remembering and imitating what they see. Through this process, they develop new behaviours and skills.

> Observational learning is based on a learner first observing then remembering and imitating what they see.

In the context of your presenting, it is helpful to identify people who role model the characteristics that you want to be able to portray and communicate. It may be that you identify a number of people who role model different attributes: some might be public figures, others might be people you know or see professionally in presentation environments.

Once you have identified suitable role models, take the time to observe them as much as you can when they present. For public figures, online video is a useful resource. As you observe them, make notes about what you notice in terms of their words, voice tone and body language that help communicate the specific trait or attribute that you have identified in them.

Once you have identified specifics you can begin to imitate these, starting with your own rehearsals for upcoming presentations. In this way you can practise developing new approaches and behaviours safely. The benefit of this practice is enhanced if you can have it recorded or observed by someone you trust to gain feedback on how you come across.

Manage your own state when you present

You need to be in a resourceful (positive, helpful) state yourself if you are seeking to manage others' perceptions of you when you are presenting.

Presenting is an activity where many people can experience a situational lack of confidence and this needs to be addressed if you are to successfully apply new ways of behaving and presenting. If you are confident when you are presenting you are more able to adapt and flex your style than if you are concerned or anxious.

Part 4 of this book, 'Delivering with maximum impact', will provide you with practical tools to create the situational confidence that you need to support your behavioural flexibility.

Be open to different ways of presenting

Each of us has our own particular style and approach to presenting. We might prepare in a certain way, have our own rituals before we stand up to speak, feel a certain way about presenting and display any number of specific characteristics and behaviours that, together, provide our audience with an impression of who we are as a person and what we stand for.

It is important to know that, at the very heart of these individual characteristics that we possess as a presenter, are habits that we have been developing and refining over many years. These habits have, in some way, served us well. We often create habits as coping strategies for the activities we engage in and we create them unconsciously. Once we have a habit, we rarely question it because we are often not even aware of it; it simply becomes 'something that we do'.

For you to be fully effective in managing the perception others have of you, you need to become aware of these presenting habits, question whether they support or hinder you in achieving your desired outcomes, and be able to change them by being open to preparing and presenting differently. Changing long-standing habits requires awareness of the habits, desire to change and the knowledge of what to do instead. But it also requires perseverance.

> Changing long-standing habits requires awareness of the habits, desire to change and the knowledge of what to do instead.

This book will provide you with many tools, techniques and approaches based on what it is that highly effective presenters do. For you to be effective in applying these tools you need to overcome the discomfort that often accompanies learning something new or changing long-standing habits.

Exercise

Pick up your pen and sign your name on a piece of paper, just as you would sign a letter.

Now put your pen in your non-preferred hand and sign your name again.

How did you experience that? It is likely that the first time you signed your name it felt natural, easy and you probably did not need to think consciously about it. That is how habits feel. When you change hands and the pen is in your non-preferred hand you probably needed to put a lot more conscious attention on the activity, it would have felt uncomfortable and you may not have been totally satisfied with the result. That is how it feels when you are trying to change your habits. Even making small changes and adjustments to how you do things can feel uncomfortable and the tendency when you do not get the result that you want (even though you know logically that the new behaviour or approach will need more practice to develop) is to revert to your old habits.

Being open to different ways of presenting requires you to understand that habit change can take time and practice before the new approaches are 'in the muscle'.

SUMMARY

▌ Be clear about how you want to be perceived by others: specify the descriptive words you would want others to use in describing you as a presenter.

▌ Only seek to develop characteristics that feel authentic to you.

▌ Look for presenters who role model the traits and characteristics that you want to demonstrate and observe what it is that they do that communicates the desired trait(s).

▌ Manage your own state in order to develop new traits and behaviours – see Chapter 12.

▌ Understand that managing perceptions requires you to change some of your presenting habits and that this may take time and will require practice!

Part

2

Preparing with the audience in mind

Preparation fundamentals

t was Benjamin Franklin who said that 'By failing to prepare, you are preparing to fail', and those words are particularly true in the context of planning for, and delivering, a presentation.

We believe that failing to engage in effective planning and preparation is almost criminally negligent for a leader in today's business environment. When the stakes are high and the outcome of your presentation is important, it is your planning and preparation that can make the difference between success and failure: it can be a critical success factor.

> **'By failing to prepare, you are preparing to fail.'**

The importance of effective preparation is easier to relate to if you consider the cost of failure.

Exercise

Consider a few presentations you have given in the past as a leader or presentations you have been in the audience for when someone else was presenting as a leader.

For each of these presentations, consider the following questions:

▶

1. What was the desired outcome of the presenter – what did they want to happen as a result of the presentation? This is likely to be connected with gaining the audience's commitment to something (perhaps motivating them to take action), imparting knowledge or information effectively, or building understanding.

2. What would have been the benefit to the business of achieving a successful outcome? Be specific and think in terms of hard (revenue and profit, etc.) as well as softer (competitive edge, morale, shared commitment, understanding, knowledge, etc.) benefits.

3. What would have been the cost to the business of not achieving a successful outcome? Be specific and think in terms of hard costs (lost revenues, profit, etc.) as well as softer (reduced competitive edge, reduced morale, motivation or commitment, etc.) costs.

4. What are the other benefits or costs associated with a successful or unsuccessful presentation? There might be secondary effects as a result of achieving or failing against the primary objective. For example, if the presenter failed to motivate a group to take action, there might be a secondary cost in decreased general morale leading to a lower work rate or higher churn of staff.

Putting values and costs against succeeding or failing in achieving the objectives of a presentation brings to the fore the importance of effective planning and preparation. Why then do so many people fail to prepare? The following are the two reasons we hear most often.

'I am fine with winging it'

The habit of 'winging it' may well have resulted from presentations that have achieved the desired outcome in the past without investing in planning. It may be that your confidence in presenting contributes to a belief that 'it will all work out well' or that your charisma will win through and secure the objective. What are the potential pitfalls of 'winging it'?

- You misread the audience's feelings, motivations or thoughts about what you are presenting or asking for from them in terms of action.
- You go into the presentation without a clear or specific objective.
- You are unprepared to answer questions that arise.
- Your presentation lacks structure and so confuses the audience.
- You are seen by the audience as unprepared, which can negatively impact your credibility with them.
- You increase the chance of failing to achieve your objectives!

'I don't have time to prepare'

It is a reality for most people that they are time pressured at work. The challenge with planning and preparation for a presentation is that it lacks an urgency that most client-facing work has and so it is easy to justify not doing it. Stephen Covey, the American author, businessman and speaker, articulates the challenge in his book *The 7 Habits of Highly Effective People*. In it he makes a distinction between tasks that are urgent (need to be actioned immediately) and those that are not urgent (can be put off). In addition to its urgency, a task can also be classified as either important (in that it takes you towards achieving an important outcome) or not important. These two criteria of urgency and importance give rise to a four-box model.

Covey states that tasks which are both urgent and important are often about delivering a result. They have to get done and they are important to the business. Tasks which are important but not urgent are those things that we know we should do but that lack the direct urgency that is often needed if we are to act. These tasks often relate to building capability.

In Covey's model, the task of delivering the presentation is directly related to *achieving a result*: we are presenting because we want or need to achieve something. The planning and preparation elements are not urgent but they are important. They are about *building our capability* to deliver the result. Because we all have tasks that are urgent and important as well as a number of tasks that we respond to because of their urgency rather than their importance (urgent but unimportant tasks) it is too easy to not make the time for planning and preparation.

If you deliver a successful presentation without putting in the planning time and you get away with it, it reinforces your belief that you don't need to make the time in future. The problem with continually choosing not to make planning and preparation for your presentations a priority, is that you are impacting your capability over time and compromising the chances of achieving a successful outcome. As a leader, this cannot be allowed to happen. Do not wait for the one important presentation when your lack of focus on planning and preparation leads to you not achieving the outcome you want. At that point you will fully experience the importance of building capability but it will be too late!

> Do not wait for the one important presentation when your lack of focus on planning and preparation leads to you not achieving the outcome you want.

What should you plan and prepare?

The reality that you might have lots of tasks and priorities competing for your time means that your planning and preparation must be both effective and efficient. Not all of your presentations will require, or even benefit from, lengthy planning and preparation. Some might require just a few minutes' thought and a focus on two or three key fundamentals. As the stakes for your presentation increase (the potential cost or benefit in whatever terms are important, be they financial or people focused) then it is highly likely that more time spent thinking about the presentation will yield benefits and increase your chances of success.

In Chapter 5 we detail a proven six-step preparation process that can be used for any presentation you are planning to deliver. But what are the key questions that you should answer for *all* presentations that you deliver? What should you focus on if you find yourself needing to give a presentation at short notice? What if you really don't have time to prepare fully?

What do I want to achieve as a result of this presentation?

It surprises us how many of the people we work with go into a presentation without first getting really clear about what their desired outcome is. Knowing what you want to achieve as a result of your presentation will guide every aspect of it and it helps to be as specific as you can in defining your desired outcome.

Ask yourself this question: 'At the end of this presentation, what specifically do I want my audience to know, be able to do or commit to?'

Why should my audience care?

Once you are clear on what your desired outcome is for the presentation you need to answer the question that will be foremost in the mind of each person in your audience: 'Why should I care?'

People buy ideas emotionally first and then justify their decisions logically, but all too often we see presenters focus exclusively on the logical argument behind their point of view.

Take the time to consider the personal 'What's In It For Me?' for your audience. It is important to put yourself in their shoes to answer this question. Rather than consider what you think makes this a compelling or important topic for them, consider their reality and what would make this topic, or achieving your desired outcome around the topic, relevant and motivating to them. This compelling 'What's In It For Me?' must be included early on in your presentation if you are to be sure to engage them emotionally so that they listen to your point of view.

> Take the time to consider the personal 'What's In It For Me?'

What do they feel about this right now?

Unless the audience is knocking at your door at the moment asking to do whatever it is that you are trying to achieve through your presentation it is likely that you need to influence them. This requires you to first understand how they feel relative to your desired outcome and to acknowledge that, before you attempt to lead them towards your goal for the presentation.

This concept is called 'pacing' and it is so important to successful presenting that we devote Chapter 6 to it.

If you only have limited time to prepare then ask yourself the following:

▊ How does this topic fit into my current reality and priorities as an audience member? How much (or little) do I care about it right now?

▊ If I were a member of the audience, how would I be *feeling* about this topic at the very start of the presentation?

▌ As an audience member, what individual descriptive
   words would summarise my feelings about this topic or the
   outcome you have in mind for the presentation?

Plan to acknowledge these possible feelings at the start of
your presentation. Remember not to specify these as how
they *must* be feeling (because you cannot know that for sure)
but rather that you could understand how some people *may*
be feeling this way.

If I were them, what questions would I have?

Often, a presentation has an opportunity for the audience to
ask questions. Even if specific time is not allowed for this
it is highly likely that your audience will have questions
in their mind. To maximise the chance of achieving your
desired outcome for the presentation take some time to
consider and write down the questions you think it likely
that members of the audience will have about the topic and
ensure that your presentation answers them.

What are my key points or messages?

When you are clear on your desired outcome and have
considered the audience, turn your attention to identifying
the key points that you want to make. It is important for
you to be able to summarise your key points succinctly and
clearly. Ideally, come up with no more than three key points.
Ensure that you articulate these at the beginning and again at
the end of your presentation.

What is the simplest and most impactful way to make my points or communicate my messages?

All too often it is easy to approach a presentation with a
PowerPoint slide deck that formed the basis of a previous
presentation and change it so that it is 'fit for purpose'.

For any presentation that you give it is worth questioning your approach to ensure that your key points are made in a simple and effective way. The following questions will help:

▌ What creative metaphor, analogy or story would help communicate my points or message?

▌ What would someone I admire as a presenter do to communicate these points or messages?

▌ What are all of my options, other than through presentation software such as PowerPoint, to deliver this presentation effectively?

▌ What images, exercises or discussions will help the audience relate to the content and messages I need to deliver?

The theme of all of these questions is around ensuring your presentation is audience centric rather than presenter centric. By asking yourself these questions and spending a little time considering the answers, any presentation that you give will be better prepared and more likely to achieve your desired outcome.

Focus on controlling the controllable

Often as a leader we are in situations where we need to influence an audience in circumstances that are not perfectly suited to the outcome that we want to achieve. In the mind of our audience will often be the issues, frustrations or reasons why something we might be proposing will not work. As most of your presentations will require people to either think or act differently as a result you need to be able to deal with the reality of an imperfect environment.

As part of your planning for any presentation you need to think about what the barriers or interferences might be for the audience that might hinder you achieving your desired outcome. Once you have identified the interferences you can categorise them into two groups: those that can be controlled or influenced in some way by either the audience or yourself and those over which you and they have no control or reasonable influence.

> Think about what the barriers or interferences might be for the audience that might hinder you achieving your desired outcome.

In your presentation, it is important to acknowledge what interferences exist that might hinder your desired outcome as your audience is probably already aware of them and are thinking about them! Often, however, your audience may be focusing on *all* of the interferences or perhaps the ones that they find most frustrating, without thinking about what is in their control or influence. This kind of thinking can be unhelpful as it is literally a waste of time focusing on things you cannot influence or control, even if they are real barriers or interferences.

Where there are real barriers or interferences, the task of a leader is to first acknowledge them and then focus attention on the things that can be controlled or influenced.

Example

Sarah has been tasked with focusing her team on delivering outstanding customer service levels and wants to set out her desires and expectations around this in a presentation. She knows that the internal computer systems make it difficult for her team to access both customer and product details at the same time. A new system is planned but won't be available for another six months. Her team have been getting frustrated and she is concerned as to how her presentation will land.

▶

The computer system issues are a real interference. By avoiding this in her presentation Sarah runs the risk of being seen by her team as unrealistic. It is likely that questions will be raised by the team about such an issue. Sarah needs to acknowledge the issue and its impact early on as it will be on the minds of her people. By clarifying that the system is an issue, that it will be replaced but that there is nothing we can do for the next few months, she can encourage her team to focus on what is possible now. Sarah's acknowledgment of the issue and her clear direction to focus on what they can control will enable her team to feel that their concerns have been heard and to now focus on controlling the controllable.

SUMMARY

▌ Planning and preparation can make the difference between success and failure in a presentation – especially in high-stakes presentations.

▌ Having achieved success in the past by 'winging it' is no excuse not to plan and prepare.

▌ Answering a few important planning questions will increase the chance of success for any presentation.

▌ Get clear on the specific objectives for the presentation: what are the outcomes you want to achieve?

▌ Consider why the outcomes you have set should be important to the audience: why should they care?

▌ Think about how they feel about the topic and your desired outcomes right now. Acknowledging this will demonstrate empathy.

▌ Give thought to what questions your audience might have and how you would answer them.

▌ Define what the key points of your presentation are. Ideally, come up with no more than three key points.

▌ Consider how you can communicate your key points to maximum effect: be creative and don't rely on presentation software.

▌ Identify what interferences might be in the minds of your audience and be prepared to acknowledge these in your presentation.

▌ Help your audience focus on those interferences that they can control, rather than dwelling on things over which they have no control or influence.

A six-step process for preparation

How you approach preparing for a presentation will be informed by a number of elements. These might include how much time you have, how important you feel the presentation is, how well you know and understand the audience and the nature and content of the presentation. One thing that impacts us all when we approach preparation is our natural, unconscious habits and preferences. These habits will lead some of us to focus mainly on the content, others on the structure and still others on not making the time to prepare at all.

It is helpful to have a structured process to support your preparation. A process helps ensure that you cover all of the important aspects of preparation and not just those that appeal to you or those you find easiest. Another benefit of following a process for preparation is that you can use it to reflect on your own performance at each step and raise your awareness as to where you need to focus more time and effort to further improve your presenting.

> A process helps ensure that you cover all of the important aspects of preparation and not just those that appeal to you or those you find easiest.

Presentation options

Before detailing a process it is helpful to consider some
of the options that you have available to communicate a
message in a face-to-face environment. All too often we can
think of presenting as a formal event – likely to involve a
laptop and some slides – where the presenter is providing
input to the audience in a similar way to a teacher in a
classroom. But there are many other options that we would
benefit from being aware of as we approach the important
task of planning.

▍ **Formal, presenter led:** It may be that a presentation, with
or without slides, where you as the presenter provide input
on content to an audience who predominantly listen and
possibly ask questions is the most appropriate approach to
meeting your objective.

▍ **Informal, presenter led:** A more informal approach might
include presenter-led discussions without a formal
structure to the presentation where you are looking to
create a dialogue or seek to address issues that arise from
the audience, rather than communicate some specific
messages.

▍ **Interactive:** A more interactive approach might include
exercises as well as discussions, possibly with the audience
helping to form the agenda and contribute to the content
itself through their input.

▍ **Facilitation:** This approach focuses more on the needs of
the audience than on the presenter dictating the content
and direction. Facilitation is helpful when you want to
engage an audience in taking responsibility for the
outcome of the session. Examples of where facilitation
can be helpful include identifying solutions to problems
that might span different departments, empowering a
group to take responsibility for how they implement a

new process or work approach and improving team-working within a department. With a facilitated approach there is less input to give and more ownership by the audience.

▍**Creative:** Presentations do not need to be limited to the delivery of structured messages. Storytelling, creative drawing and working together actively on a situation (rather than being part of a presentation *about* a situation) can all deliver results. Examples of this approach include a 'Sword and Shield' exercise where you draw representations of what you stand for or what you feel are strengths and weakness of the team, use of creative metaphors to encourage wider and more creative thinking or asking groups to create presentations themselves using multimedia (video, photographs, magazines, etc.)

While planning is important whatever approach you choose, you do need to be open to all of the possibilities if you are to maximise the chance of success and plan accordingly.

What follows is a six-step process for preparation. You can utilise it for any presentation that you give: formal or informal, facilitated or input led, structured or unstructured.

Six-step process

The following process gives six chronological steps to ensure that you include everything necessary for effective preparation. It is easy to apply and will improve the quality and outcome of any presentation. Depending on the nature of the presentation you can either go into detail on each step or simply use it to prompt some thoughts.

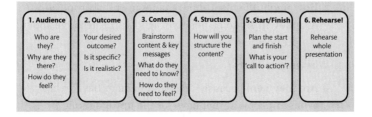

1. Know your audience

Preparation must start with considering your audience. How they feel about the topic, what their reality is and their mix (in terms of seniority, job role, responsibilities and knowledge, for example) are all critical considerations if your message is to be well received, especially if you are seeking to influence their behaviour.

Key questions to consider about the audience are:

▌ Who are they?

 ▌ Who will be in the audience and how many people?

 ▌ What is their level or range of seniority?

 ▌ What is their understanding about the topic I am to present on?

 ▌ Do I know them? If not, is it appropriate for me to speak with them (or some of them) prior to the presentation?

▌ How do they feel?

 ▌ What are their feelings and emotions likely to be at present? What are their daily challenges or frustrations that it would help me to be aware of?

 ▌ How might they feel about me? Are they likely to be positive, agnostic or negative towards me?

▌ How might they feel about the topic or my proposition?
Are they likely to be positive, agnostic or negative about
the proposition?

▌ Why are they here?

　▌ Are they here because they want to be or have to be?
What impact will that have for the presentation?

▌ What do they need if I am to succeed?

　▌ What do I need to address if the audience are to be both
willing and able to support achieving my outcome for the
presentation?

Linked with this last question 'What do they need if I am to
succeed?' is an understanding that behaviour change, which
is often what you are looking to create through your
presentations, is dependent on a number of factors.

The Logical Levels of Change model, attributed to the
anthropologist Gregory Bateson and developed by Robert B.
Dilts, is a useful way of considering what your audience
might need:

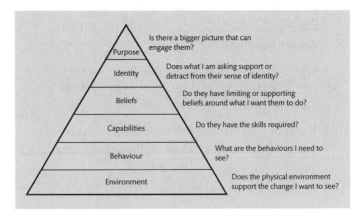

The Logical Levels of Change

By considering your audience against this model you can help identify what their needs are that might need to be met if you are to achieve the desired result.

Starting at the bottom of the triangle you can consider what questions your audience might need answered:

▌ **Environment:** This looks at the 'where', 'when' and 'with whom' questions that surround what you are looking to achieve. To what extent does the environment support what you are looking to achieve? This might be the physical environment, the opportunities, the team, etc.

▌ **Behaviour:** This is about 'what do I need them to do relative to what they are doing now?' What are the behaviours I need them to engage in and how are they performing relative to those behaviours now?

▌ **Capabilities:** This is the 'how?' and often relates to the skills and capabilities that might be needed relative to the existing skills and behaviours being demonstrated: do they have the required skills and capabilities?

▌ **Beliefs:** Beliefs are an important factor for change in many situations. This is about questions such as 'why should I change?' and 'do I believe that change is possible?' For change to occur, individuals need to believe that it is possible for them and that it fits with their personal values.

▌ **Identity:** Does what I am asking fit with the audience's sense of 'who they are' as individuals or as a team?

▌ **Purpose:** Does what I am asking fit with the audience's sense of purpose? This is about answering questions such as 'what for?' and 'what is this in service of?'

If your presentation is high-stakes you might consider lobbying your audience in advance to build credibility, connection and understanding with them. Two ways in which you can do this are:

▌ **Arrange individual conversations:** It may be appropriate to either meet or telephone either all or some of the audience to gauge their feelings and needs around the presentation you are to give. If you have a large audience it is often helpful to have conversations with a cross-section of the people who will be in attendance so that you have a representation of the views that will be present.

▌ **Implement a survey:** It is increasingly easy to administer an online survey to elicit views from the audience in advance of a presentation. This can be set up so that responses are either anonymous or attributed to individuals depending on the nature of the topic.

A significant benefit of gaining an objective understanding of the audience and how they are feeling about the topic before you present is that it will enable you to create suitable pacing statements (see Chapter 6) to help ensure that you demonstrate the empathy necessary if you want to lead them to a different point of view through your presentation.

2. Identify your desired outcome

Once you have considered your audience, how they feel and what their needs might be, you need to get clear about the specific outcome that you want to achieve for the presentation.

Defining specifically what you want to achieve from the presentation brings a number of benefits:

▌ It guides your thinking about the content needed to achieve the outcome.

▌ It enables you to consider how realistic achieving your outcome is in the time available for your presentation and in light of how the audience are likely to be feeling, so that you can plan accordingly.

▮ It creates a focus for everything else in your planning to ensure you pay attention to the right things.

Your outcome should be specific, measurable and realistic. It is likely to help you define and focus on a call to action: defining what you want participants to be able to know or do as a result of the presentation.

Most presentations will have an objective that is built around one or more of three alternative outcomes: 'By the end of this presentation, the audience will...:

▮ ...be able to... (be equipped in order to make a choice);

▮ ...commit to... (make a commitment to a specific action);

▮ ...understand...' (have knowledge and/or understanding).

In creating your outcome you must take account of how your audience is likely to be feeling relative to your topic and desired outcome at the very start of your presentation. Focusing on your audience will enable you to be much more realistic and might result in you changing your outcome accordingly. While you might want to achieve a significant outcome you must recognise that your audience will buy into your ideas, information or proposition emotionally first and then justify it logically. By paying attention to their likely emotions you increase the chance of developing a presentation that makes the maximum positive impact.

3. Brainstorm content and key messages

In a busy working environment we may have been guilty in the past of creating a presentation by taking a slide deck from a previous and somewhat similar presentation and changing a few of the details. While this is likely to save some preparation time and might actually work in some instances it is often a bad idea.

If you have done a good job of considering your audience and then creating a realistic and focused outcome you are now able to start thinking about what you will include in terms of content.

There are two elements to consider:

▌ What content will support your messaging?

▌ What are your key messages or themes?

Content to support your messaging

While in some situations the choice of content for your presentation might be obvious, it is a good idea to question the obvious choices in light of your knowledge of the audience and the outcome you have set.

> It is a good idea to question the obvious choices in light of your knowledge of the audience and the outcome you have set.

We recommend using a brainstorming approach to gather your ideas before funnelling these ideas down into the content that will be most relevant and useful. Taking this approach will also enable you to consider what is the best way to get the message across effectively (for example, through teaching, facilitating, creating exercises, etc.). This brainstorming can be done either in a group or on your own, but it helps to follow a few guidelines to get the most from the process:

1. Set a time limit for the brainstorming phase. A limited time for brainstorming encourages you to get ideas out quickly.

2. Having considered the audience and your desired outcome for the presentation you can now simply write down any

and all ideas that come to mind. Suspend critical judgement as quantity is more important than quality at this stage. You will be able to refine and choose from your ideas later.

3. It often helps to have a big sheet of paper with your objective written in the middle and then create a spider diagram with key ideas coming out from your objective. This gives you the ability to connect ideas and define themes, making it easier to structure the presentation later.

4. Once you have completed the brainstorming phase you are likely to be faced with lots of ideas and possibilities for content: ideas, metaphors, key points and maybe some questions to consider – remember, in the brainstorming phase you are capturing everything and anything that comes to mind. The focus now is to funnel all of these ideas into the key content that must be included in the presentation and begin to think about how it can be logically grouped. If you have created a spider diagram you may already have some content groupings.

5. When selecting content you need to hold in the front of your mind the amount of time you have available for the presentation. It is a common failing for presenters to try to utilise too much content for the time available in the presentation. Keeping the time limit in mind will help you focus on selecting the most relevant content.

Key messages or themes

Now you have an idea of the content it is helpful, both for the audience and for yourself, to create some key messages or themes. Information is much more memorable if it is grouped and we provide more information on this in Part 3.

Once you have defined the key messages or themes and linked the content you want to cover to each of them, ensuring it fits within your available time, you can think about how to structure the information.

4. Structure the content

We provide much more information on this important stage of your planning and preparation in Part 3.

Your structure needs to be easy to understand for the audience and have some logic or reason for the progression of content. It is likely to be informed by the key themes of your presentation with content grouped within each theme. Ensuring that information is clearly structured and signposting this structure during your presentation provides the clarity your audience will be looking for.

> Ensuring that information is clearly structured and signposting this structure during your presentation provides the clarity your audience will be looking for.

5. Focus on the start and finish

People remember most easily the first things you say and the last things you say in a presentation. This is due to the primacy and recency effects that have been well researched, and it means that you must pay particular attention to planning the opening of your presentations and the closing of them.

> You must pay particular attention to planning the opening of your presentations and the closing of them.

What should you include in almost every presentation at the start and the end to maximise the effectiveness of communicating your messages? There is more information on the detail behind what we summarise below in Part 3.

At the start

At the start of your presentation you are looking to:

- create a strong positive impact;
- engage the audience early on;
- communicate empathy early on;
- build the 'Why?', the 'What's In It For Me?' (WIIFM) for the audience to connect with their motivation;
- give clarity around your expectations for the presentation;
- where appropriate, summarise your key messages and desired outcome for the presentation.

Here are some practical things to cover at the start of your presentation in a suggested chronological order. All of these are covered in more detail in Part 3:

- Plan a strong opening statement to gain immediate audience attention. Known as a 'spike', this might be a question or a statement that compels attention.
- Pace the audience to build empathy. Create some statements that the audience can agree with and that demonstrate your understanding of their feelings, views and needs.
- Summarise the purpose of your presentation, your objectives for it and your key points or themes (this is called signposting) and the agenda.
- Give your credentials. If the audience do not know you, it is important to set out what gives you the right to be speaking on the topic. Summarise your background and relevant experience.
- Give the audience information on:
  - how long the presentation will last;
  - how you will handle questions (as and when they arise or at the end);

▌ your expectations for the audience (whether you want them to interact, engage in group discussions, etc.?)

At the end

At the conclusion of your presentation you are looking to:

▌ leave the audience feeling positively predisposed to your argument (if appropriate);

▌ maximise the chance that they will remember your key points;

▌ manage their emotional state so that they leave feeling positive;

▌ engage them with a clear 'call to action': i.e. what you want them to do as a result of the presentation.

Here are a few things to cover to maximise your chance of achieving the points listed above:

▌ Summarise your key messages or themes again.

▌ Give a strong and confident 'call to action'.

▌ Ensure that you 'have the last word'. If you handle questions towards the end of your presentation, ensure that you answer these before you go into your final summary of the key points and call to action. This will better enable you to manage how the audience feels at the end of the presentation. See Part 4 for more information on this.

6. Rehearse!

This final stage of the planning and preparation process is perhaps the most important. It surprises us how many senior leaders fail to rehearse their presentations. Could you imagine an actor going on stage for the first night of a new play without having exhaustively rehearsed his lines and his delivery? And yet often we see leaders engaging in high-stakes presentations where the audience are witnessing his or her first rehearsal!

> Could you imagine an actor going on stage for the first night of a new play without having exhaustively rehearsed his lines and his delivery?

Some practical tips to get the most from rehearsing your presentation are:

- If possible, rehearse in the location that you will be delivering the presentation in.

- Rehearse all the way through. We see lots of leaders who rehearse only the first part of their presentation but have never had a complete run-through.

- If possible, record on video the rehearsal and play it back to see how you come across.

- If appropriate and possible, ask someone to watch the rehearsal so that they can give effective feedback to you on how you come across, the pace and confidence of your delivery, the clarity of your messages and the degree to which you engage them.

- Notice what you need in order to deliver the messages most effectively while being able to engage with the audience. When you rehearse, be aware of how much time you spend looking at notes and consider what you need to do to ensure you connect with the audience rather than your notes. Some people have cue cards with a summary of each key point or individual words to aid their memory about what they will be covering.

SUMMARY

▌ Having a structured process for your preparation helps ensure you cover everything you need to.

▌ Consider what form your presentation should take to maximise the chance of achieving your objectives: formal, informal, facilitated, creative, etc.

▌ Follow the six-step preparation process:

1. Know your audience.

2. Identify your desired outcome.

3. Brainstorm content and key messages.

4. Structure the content.

5. Focus on the start and finish.

6. Rehearse!

6
Pacing the audience

The big mistake: trying to lead your audience too quickly

Have you ever attended a presentation where you felt interested in the topic but disconnected from the presenter? Perhaps you felt that they didn't fully appreciate your needs and views or were pushing their ideas a little too hard at you. It may be that you felt they were almost too enthusiastic about their message or that they lacked the necessary context to ensure that their message felt relevant to you.

What is going on in these situations? What is the presenter either doing or not doing that is contributing to a sense of disconnection between them and the audience?

What often happens is that a presenter tries to lead their audience too quickly to the points they are trying to make or the feelings they want their audience to have. In doing this, the presenter creates a sense in the audience that they do not fully understand their needs or 'get' them. Trying to lead your audience too quickly is an easy mistake to make: one that is all too common among leaders. It is also an easy thing to prevent through the application of some simple yet effective techniques. This chapter will show you how to avoid making a mistake that can have a significant negative impact on your presentations.

What is 'leading too early'?

Have you ever been in a situation where someone was angry or frustrated with you for either something you had done or not done in either your personal or professional life? Perhaps they came to confront you with it and your reaction was to softly say 'calm down'. What was the impact of those two softly spoken words in response to someone's obvious frustration? It is likely that it did not help or defuse the situation at all. In fact it is likely to have escalated it. Why? Because there was a clear gap between how the other person was feeling and the feelings that you were demonstrating, resulting in the other person feeling that you did not 'get' the importance of the situation to them. Your intention was to lead the conversation into calmer waters, but by not demonstrating that you understood how important this issue was to the other person you showed a gap. This is an example of 'leading too early'.

As a leader you will often be presenting on topics where you want to engage your audience and leave them feeling positive or motivated about your message. It is likely that in a number of these situations you will already be feeling genuinely positive about what you have to say and it is with this feeling that you start your presentation. Even if you do not communicate your thoughts and feelings explicitly in the words that you say, they are likely to be communicated very clearly through your body language and the way you speak your words.

Enthusiasm for your message is great to have. In fact we would highly recommend it! The problem is that your audience may not feel the same. The reality is that there is likely to be quite a gap between how you feel about your message or proposition and how your audience feels about it at the start of your presentation.

> The reality is that there is likely to be quite a gap between how you feel about your message or proposition and how your audience feels about it at the start of your presentation.

This difference in how your audience feels at the start of your presentation compared to how you feel is where we can lose a presentation right at the very start. Because people buy ideas emotionally first and then justify them logically, this 'emotional gap' is critical to recognise (if it exists) and address before you seek to lead the audience towards your desired position. If you do not acknowledge how the audience might be feeling before you start into the body of your presentation they will only see how *you* feel, what *your* emotions are, and this can potentially communicate a number of things to the audience:

- a lack of understanding by you of how they really feel;
- a disconnect, or gap, between how you feel as the leader or presenter and how they feel;
- a feeling that you are not aware of the reality that they face; their concerns, pressures or challenges.

By not acknowledging first how the audience might be feeling or what they might be thinking you are leading them too quickly.

The reason that this is such a big mistake is that people need to feel acknowledged and heard before they are willing to

follow us. When people feel heard they are more likely to
listen.

> **When people feel heard they are more
> likely to listen.**

What is pacing?

Pacing is a simple and powerful technique to communicate
to your audience that you understand something of their
current reality, of how they might be thinking and feeling
about the topic you are about to present on. It is something
you can both plan to do at the start of your presentations and
something that you can utilise 'in the moment' if you find
that there is a gap between how your audience feels about
your proposition or message and how you feel and need
them to feel in order to take the relevant action. It is nearly
always useful to incorporate some element of pacing in your
presentations, but some situations will require more pacing
than others. As a general rule, the bigger the potential gap
in your thinking and feelings at the start of a presentation
compared with how the audience might be thinking or
feeling, the more pacing you should engage in.

> **Some situations will require more pacing
> than others.**

The objective of pacing is to ensure that your audience feels
heard and understood before you start to lead them. It is
important that you acknowledge and communicate this
without telling them how they feel. The reality is you are
unlikely to know exactly how they are feeling unless they tell
you; but, by taking some time to put yourself in their shoes
and consider their environment, challenges and concerns,
you can imagine what they *may* be thinking and feeling. The
exercise on 'Awareness: taking different perspectives' in
Chapter 2 can help develop this empathy.

Once you have considered how your audience might be thinking and feeling you can construct some statements that acknowledge these possibilities. You are seeking to create statements that:

▌ elicit nods of agreement from some of your audience;

▌ reference their possible current reality;

▌ acknowledge any major concerns that they might have;

▌ demonstrate that you have considered their views.

Pacing is not about delivering any of your content, it is about earning the right to deliver your content through demonstrating understanding of the audience.

> ▌ Pacing is not about delivering any of your content, it is about earning the right to deliver your content through demonstrating understanding of the audience.

How much pacing should you do?

Because the emotional engagement of your audience is so critical to achieving your desired outcome it is important that you do enough pacing for your audience to feel heard and understood. This will vary with the audience, the topic and the situation but there is a general rule that is helpful here:

Pace. . .Pace. . .Lead. . .

It is important to give enough time to pacing the audience at the start of a presentation – especially if there is a large potential gap between how they feel about your topic now and how you would like them to feel. You need to spend enough time pacing and then pacing some more to earn the right to lead. Not doing this can result in an audience that feels you are glossing over their feelings and concerns, that you don't really understand them.

Example

Imagine that you are presenting to a group of disgruntled employees on yet another change programme that the corporate head office is implementing. They have been through many of these recently and some are resentful of yet another change in how they work. They see the new procedures as overly bureaucratic and a hindrance to getting their job done.

You know that you should use pacing and so, at the very start of the presentation to introduce this change, you mention that you know that there have been some change programmes and that these have caused some concerns. Having seen some head-nods in the audience you move on to introduce the new change. What might the audience feel about this? It is possible that they would feel you have paid lip-service to their concerns. In fact, your scant use of pacing may well reinforce the negative views of the audience.

In this situation where feelings might be running high and be quite negative you need to pace more before getting to the main content of your presentation. You might start by recognising how busy people are, acknowledging that changes have occurred, that they have created some challenges while solving others, that in the short term they might be viewed as causing more problems than they solve and that the idea of yet another change may give rise to frustration. You might then talk about the business environment and how these challenges are being faced by many companies and that it is difficult for many and that it is often challenging to change working practices.

This feels as though you have truly understood and acknowledged the possible feelings and concerns – it feels more authentic. Once you have paced the group in this way, you can then move on to speak about what the new change is and why it is important because the audience is likely to feel more genuinely listened to.

How do you do it?

Pacing is something to be done at the start of your presentations and you can plan to do this by considering two questions:

1. What do I need my audience to be feeling and thinking at the end of my presentation in order to maximise the chance of successfully achieving my objective for the presentation?

2. If I put myself in their shoes:

   a. How might they be *feeling* about this topic right now?

   b. What might they be *thinking* about this topic right now?

   c. What might their concerns be?

   d. What have they been experiencing recently that might be on their mind as I present about this topic?

This will enable you to create a few statements that you can use at the start of the presentation that communicate this thinking before you move on to your content. Remember, it is important that these statements demonstrate that you understand how they *might* be thinking and feeling without presenting them as how they *are* feeling.

Another way of pacing an audience is to create a short exercise that gets them to surface the concerns, feelings and challenges through group discussions. Pacing in this way creates a sense of co-creation that can increase buy-in when you move on to your content.

As you think about this concept of pacing it may raise the question about whether pacing could come across as negative and whether this is a good idea at any point in a presentation. Pacing is not about being negative, but rather about communicating an understanding of the real concerns and feelings that people may have. It might extend to acknowledging certain facts about their current reality. In this way it is not about presenting either a positive or negative message but one that shows thought.

Example

We were asked by an insurance company to deliver a global programme on 'Mastering the Challenging Conversations' to all of their senior managers involved in giving performance reviews. The leadership was concerned that managers were being too lenient in assessing individual performance and not engaging in robust and objective performance conversations. This meant that large bonuses were being paid not because performance was outstanding, but because managers were not holding their people accountable.

We had developed a one-day workshop with some great models and exercises and stood at the front of the room on the morning of the pilot. If this pilot went well we were to travel around the world to their hub offices to deliver the programme.

As the first two or three participants arrived, we were surprised that they did not come and shake hands but simply went and sat in their seats with no words or eye contact. It was clear as the room filled up that the group were nowhere near as motivated as we were about the day ahead and the topic of discussion. In fact, one participant did shake hands but said: 'you do realise this is a mandatory course and none of us want to be here.'

We were faced with the certainty that there was a clear gap between how this group was feeling about the workshop and how they needed to feel by the end if they were to take any action. We had to think on our feet and construct some effective pacing – urgently.

We chose to do this by starting the workshop summarising a variety of views that participants might have had. These included acknowledging that it was mandatory and so there may be some resentment at having to be here, that they might not have seen the importance of the topic, and so on. We then asked a question of the group: 'On a scale of 1-10, where 10 is "excited" and 1 is "not looking forward to this", what score would you give yourself?' We asked for a show of hands and were dismayed (but not surprised) that the first hand went up at 3! This pacing allowed us to acknowledge the feelings in the room and communicate that we understood. Through this acknowledgement, we were then able to ask participants to focus on what they could control in a day that was mandatory: their willingness to learn something of value.

While the group was not the most positive or motivated that we have ever worked with, they did engage in our material because we took the time to pace them first.

SUMMARY

▌ A common mistake that presenters make is trying to lead their audience too quickly.

▌ You often feel motivated about your proposition but the audience may not feel the same: there may be a gap that needs to be bridged.

▌ People need to feel that you understand where they are now (and how they might be feeling now) before being open to you leading them to where you want them to be.

▌ Pacing is acknowledging how the audience might be feeling about your topic or presentation.

▌ You can pace by making statements at the start of your presentation to which you are likely to get a 'yes' response from the audience.

▌ Pace. . .pace. . .lead: you need to spend enough time pacing the audience to ensure they feel understood and acknowledged.

▌ Plan to utilise pacing statements at the start of your presentation to earn the right to lead the audience towards your desired outcome.

Part

3

Structuring your message

Why structure is so important and the key principles

Why is structure so important?

Think back now to a time when you sat through a presentation that lacked structure. What were your feelings about the presentation and the presenter? What do you recall about the content and key messages now? How did you feel at the end of the presentation?

Presentations that lack structure often appear rambling, unfocused and disorganised. Worse, we conflate the presentation and how we feel about it with the presenter and make judgements that can have a long-lasting, negative impact on our views of the individual who presented.

> Presentations that lack structure often appear rambling, unfocused and disorganised.

Structure is absolutely critical if your presentations are to be coherent, organised, interesting and clear. They need to have a clear flow that the audience can relate to, understand and that supports them taking in the information you wish to impart.

If your presentation is an opportunity to influence, the lack of a clear and appropriate structure risks losing that opportunity.

Organising and structuring your information, such as categorising it into subsets, or chunks, makes it much easier for the audience to file the information away for future recall. When we are being presented to we expect the presenter to have thought carefully about how to organise and communicate their information to aid our understanding and keep us interested.

What can we learn from storytelling?

Storytelling is the oldest form of communicating information and creating an emotional journey for the listener. Creating a narrative through your presentation will connect the audience with your content and, when carefully planned and executed, change their emotional state.

Think about a good story. It has a strong sense of a beginning, a middle and an end. Stories often draw us in with characters that we can relate to and might have various twists and turns to keep us engaged before building to a climax. As we read a story from a great author we might become aware of how their choice of words and the thread of the narrative bring about emotional transitions for us. We might experience a number of different emotions before we finish the book, all created by the structure and word choice of the author.

> Creating a narrative through your presentation will connect the audience with your content and, when carefully planned and executed, change their emotional state.

Whatever the 'journey' is that you want your presentations to engage people with, having a clear and relevant structure will be at the heart of your success.

Key principles

As a leader, you will need to create and deliver a variety of presentations to different audiences. Some might be updating people with information while others might require you to achieve some high-stakes outcomes and engage an audience to commit to something that could have a substantial impact on your business.

With this wide variety of presenting situations, what do you need to pay attention to in terms of how you structure your presentations? What are the key principles that, if applied to any presentation, can make a significant positive impact on both how the presentation is received and the chances of achieving a successful outcome?

What follows are some key principles to apply when considering the structure of any presentation. While the specifics of how you implement them will alter depending on the situation and the presentation, following these five key principles will benefit any presentation.

1. Have a compelling key message(s)

A successful presentation ideally has a clear and compelling key message that the audience can understand and engage with. While it might be difficult in some presentations – particularly those where you need to deliver bad news or simply provide an information update – it is certainly worth considering the following questions which will guide other aspects of how you structure your presentation. Some of these questions will be more relevant than others depending on the situation:

▌ What, specifically, is the purpose of this presentation?

▌ What, specifically, are the key messages that I want to give to this audience?

▌ How can I appeal to the 'What's In It For Me?' for individual audience members? Why should they care about this topic?

▌ What are the positive consequences to the audience of achieving a successful outcome?

▌ What are the negative consequences to the audience of not achieving a successful outcome?

Throughout this book we have repeated the phrase 'people buy emotionally and then justify logically' as it is a key theme you need to focus on. In terms of your presentations, this means that your key messages ideally need to engage the audience at an emotional level if you are to maximise the chance of achieving success. All too often we see presenters that spend a lot of time crafting elegant logical presentations that miss this important point. Without creating true emotional engagement you are less likely to achieve the motivation to action so often required in high-stakes presentations. By answering the important 'What's In It For Me?' question from the audience's perspective, you are more likely to craft more persuasive and compelling key messages.

Research shows that messages from credible sources and messages that connect with the audience are more effective in persuading, but there are two techniques to crafting your message that will also help make them more compelling and persuasive:

1. **Use of power words.** One thing that you can do to improve how your messages are heard by others is to use, where appropriate, one or more 'power words'. Power words are words that have a positive impact on the engagement of the listener. There are five power words that you might easily be able to include in your messaging:

▌ Increase

▌ Reduce

▌ Save

▌ Solve

▌ Improve.

2. **Communicate 'benefits' rather than 'features'.** While a well-known tool for sales people, it is also one that holds very true when you need to engage and motivate people through your presentations. A feature is simply a fact, something that is true. Many presenters focus on the facts behind their message: the features. They create content which justifies the truth of what they are saying. While there is nothing wrong with communicating facts, we are missing an opportunity by not converting the feature into a benefit.

A benefit is something that is seen as relevant and beneficial by the person hearing it (and not just to you as the presenter giving the information!). To create a benefit from a feature you need to think about the audience and answer the question 'so what?'

Communicating benefits answers the question in the audience's mind: 'Why should I care?' Do not make the mistake of assuming that the audience can and will make the link from a feature to a benefit. Do it for them by crafting your key messages in benefits language.

An easy way to convert a feature into a benefit is to state the feature and then add the words '...which means that...' Completing the sentence and answering the 'which means that' statement provides a benefit.

2. The Power of 3

Most of your presentations will have a requirement to deliver certain information or messages that you want people to be able to remember and recall later. A very powerful concept that can be leveraged in your presentations to increase both impact and subsequent recall is known as the 'Power of 3'.

The Power of 3 has been used by the most effective presenters and marketers for many years. It is based on the idea that information or messages grouped into threes is inherently more memorable and persuasive than smaller or larger groupings.

> Information or messages grouped into threes is inherently more memorable and persuasive than smaller or larger groupings.

Research in 2013 by Kurt A. Carlson (Georgetown University) and Suzanne B. Shu (University of California) also found that three was the number of positive claims that should be used to produce the most positive impression of a product or service when consumers know that the message source has a persuasion motive. More claims are better until the fourth claim, at which point consumers' persuasion knowledge causes them to see all the claims with scepticism. Often, the Power of 3 can take the form of three key words that, when used together, are inherently more memorable. They can be individually descriptive or can make a phrase more memorable because it is made up of three words. As such, the Power of 3 is found in many contexts:

Marketing slogans:

- 'I'm Loving It' (McDonald's)
- 'Just Do It!' (Nike)
- 'You're Worth It' (L'Oréal)

Political messages:

▌ 'Education, education, education' (1997 UK Labour Party slogan)

▌ 'A government of the people, by the people, for the people' (Abraham Lincoln, Gettysburg Address, 1863)

▌ 'Tonight, we gather to affirm the greatness of our nation – not because of [1] the height of our skyscrapers, or [2] the power of our military, or [3] the size of our economy.' (Barack Obama, Democratic National Convention keynote speech, July 2004)

Other contexts:

▌ The three wise men (the Bible)

▌ Goldilocks and the three bears (children's story)

▌ 'Liberté, Égalité, Fraternité' (national motto of France)

▌ 'Veni, vidi, vici' (I came, I saw, I conquered) (Julius Caesar)

▌ 'Faster, Higher, Stronger' (Olympic motto)

▌ '[1] It means to try to tell your kids everything you thought you'd have the next 10 years to tell them in just a few months. [2] It means to make sure everything is buttoned up so that it will be as easy as possible for your family. [3] It means to say your goodbyes.' (Steve Jobs, Stanford Commencement address, 2005)

You can see from these examples that you can utilise the Power of 3 either by creating three individual words that represent a central idea or concept that you want the audience to engage with, or you can use it by linking three parallel elements or phrases.

When structuring your presentation, look for opportunities to incorporate the Power of 3 concept, either by distilling key concepts down to three words or by using three phrases to group your ideas and make them more memorable. Even the old adage of how to structure a presentation is a use of the Power of 3 concept: 'Tell them what you're going to tell them, tell them, tell them what you've told them.'

> 'Tell them what you're going to tell them, tell them, tell them what you've told them.'

3. Less is more ... reduce your content

How you plan for, and structure, your presentations now will be driven to a large extent by your unconscious habits and preferences. One of these habits that we have seen all too often is the inclusion of far too much content.

Presentations that include too much content can seem to the audience to be:

- rushed;
- difficult to follow;
- boring;
- overwhelming;
- too detailed.

You do not want your presentations to feel any of these things. In fact, you often need them to feel the reverse!

What is the 'right' amount of content?

The somewhat glib but honest answer to this is 'just enough for you to achieve your objective'.

The amount of content will be driven by a number of things:

- the objective of the presentation;
- the starting point of the audience, their knowledge on the topic and attitude towards it;

▌ the nature of the presentation (is it primarily about disseminating information or engaging a group with a new idea or getting them to commit to action?);

▌ the time that you have available.

Above all you need to consider content from the perspective of what your audience *needs* rather than what you *want* to include.

One option that you have and should consider when structuring your presentation is to focus it on the key messages and the content required to convey them, while having a handout that can include the more detailed information that some, but maybe not all, of your audience would like to see. In this way, you make seeing the detail an option for those who need it rather than forcing it on those who don't.

4. Use the 'Magic Number': 7$^+$/$^-$2

Some presentations do need to convey a lot of information. It may be that your presentation has quite a few specific topics to cover and maybe a few key ideas within each topic. How can you maximise the chance of your audience retaining the information you give them in these circumstances? What can you do from a structural standpoint that will help keep your audience engaged when you have greater amounts of information to convey?

In 1956, George A. Miller of Princeton University's Department of Psychology published one of the most highly cited papers in psychology. It was titled 'The Magical Number Seven, Plus or Minus Two: Some Limits on Our Capacity for Processing Information' and gives a very practical tip on how we can structure information to aid recall. He found that the number of 'slots' available in our short term memory are 7 + or − 2, i.e. between 5 and 9. These slots correspond to 'chunks' of information or individual ideas. Once we reach our limit of these new ideas in any one presentation we tend to find it more difficult to recall, often forgetting one or two of the ideas or chunks.

> Once we reach our limit of these new ideas in any one presentation we tend to find it more difficult to recall, often forgetting one or two of the ideas or chunks.

Think for a moment about how your telephone number is shown. In France, an eight-digit telephone number is often expressed as four pairs of numbers; in the UK an eleven-digit telephone number is often split into a five-digit area code and a six-digit number. This makes the number much easier to recall than a single string of either eight or eleven digits.

How can you use this concept in the structure of your presentations to make the content easier to remember and recall?

If you have a considerable amount of information that you need to convey to an audience, group it into a number of logical 'chunks' or subsets. Ensure that you are presenting your audience with, ideally, no more than six or seven points in any one part of a presentation.

Example

You have a presentation to give that will introduce a new service line that the audience will be expected to learn about and sell to their existing clients. You have an hour and a half to present and want to cover 12 main items:

1. What the new service line is
2. Its key features
3. Benefits to the customer

4. How it will be sold

5. Which customers it is most suitable for

6. The pricing structure (there are different prices for new and existing customers and for customers with certain other products)

7. What the internal processes are to set up a client with the new service line – which departments you inform and what each needs from you

8. How you use the existing internal systems to add the service at your workstation

9. What communication the client will receive as a result of signing up

10. What the technical issues are around the new service line

11. How to prevent the most common technical issues from occurring

12. What the process is for technical support

As you read down this list there is a lot to take in and it may be that your eyes have glazed over around item 6 or 7.

Using our knowledge of 'The Magic Number' we know that grouping information into smaller chunks than this single list of 12 items is likely to make it easier for the audience to consume and subsequently remember. We might, therefore, construct the agenda and the presentation in the following way:

1. The new service line

   a. Its key features

   b. Benefits to the customer

2. How it will be sold

   a. Which customers it is most suitable for

   b. The pricing structure

▶

    i. New customers

    ii. Existing customers

    iii. Existing customers with certain other products

3. What the internal processes are to set up a client with the new service line

   a. Which departments you inform and what each needs from you

   b. How you use the existing internal systems to add the service at your workstation

   c. What communication the client will receive as a result of signing up

4. What the technical issues are around the new service line

   a. How to prevent the most common technical issues from occurring

   b. What the process is for technical support

With this arrangement of content, no level of information (key heading, sub-heading or lower) has more than four elements. Notice how even using a visual indent for different grouping levels makes it easier for us to order and recall information.

Showing chunks of content in this way in the agenda for your presentation and in your signposting throughout your presentation will make it easier for your audience to understand, consume and recall the information.

5. Structure to engage and motivate the audience

We have mentioned a number of times in this book that 'people buy emotionally and justify logically'. All too often, despite this fact, we structure our presentations around the logical justification. We create presentations with data, information, charts and logical reasoning articulated in bullet points.

When you need to engage hearts and minds, motivate people to take action or gain buy-in to a new idea you have to pay attention to the emotional component of the engagement process. By structuring your presentation to take account of the emotional journey that your audience needs to travel you can dramatically increase the chance of achieving a successful outcome.

Some questions will help you define the journey that your audience needs to travel:

1. How does my audience need to feel at the end of the presentation if individuals are to take the action I desire of them?

2. Putting myself in their shoes, what words might describe how they are likely to be feeling at the start of the presentation about this topic?

Your answers to these two questions will give you an indication of the journey and will enable you to assess whether you are being realistic in your desired outcome.

Example

You have to implement a new call handling process with your customer service representatives. The new process requires staff to capture more information when they are speaking to a customer and requires them to run through some specific terms and conditions. This represents additional work compared to how they handle the calls currently. While you could simply instruct them to do this, you are keen for them to capture as much information as possible and recognise that they have the choice to either 'follow the process to a minimum level' or really engage the customer to find out useful information in addition to the minimum requirement.

▶

Your team has had a few changes in process recently and is feeling a little cynical.

By asking the two questions above you come up with the following:

1. How does my audience need to feel at the end of the presentation if individuals are to take the action I desire of them?

 ▮ committed to going beyond the 'minimum requirement' of the new process;

 ▮ motivated, positive and prepared to ask more questions and enter the information.

2. Putting myself in their shoes, what words might describe how they are likely to be feeling at the start of the presentation about this topic?

 ▮ cynical about yet more change;

 ▮ time pressured so concerned about the additional overhead required to implement this change;

 ▮ keen to maximise the quality of the relationships they have with the customers they speak to.

Clearly there is a significant difference between how they feel now about what you are going to ask them and how they need to feel in order to act in the way that you desire. Knowing this enables you to structure your presentation to a) demonstrate your empathy at the start (pacing), b) recognise the change in emotion that your presentation should seek to bring about and c) help you decide if this can be done in one presentation or whether you need to break the task down into two or more separate presentations. You can also now consider the best method to use to engage the group: this might be through a formal presentation but might alternatively be through facilitating them in a group discussion.

Awareness of the gap between how your audience feels now and how they need to feel in order to take the action you desire enables you to plan the steps to move them towards that desired state.

For example, if an audience is cynical at the start and you need them to feel positive and motivated at the end of your presentation it is unreasonable to believe that you can do this in one simple step. It is unlikely that any one thing you could do or say would help your audience make such a transition in how they feel. However, you could plan this move through four or five steps. You could use pacing to show empathy with how they might be feeling now then take steps to move them from 'cynical' to 'open to listen', and then from 'open to listen' to 'curious'. From 'curious' you might transition them to 'engaged', and from 'engaged' you might transition to 'motivated'. By breaking the journey down into steps, as illustrated in the diagram below, you can more easily structure your presentation to maximise the chance of achieving each distinct transition in feeling.

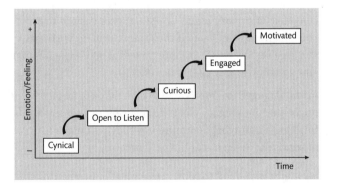

You can plan specific elements of your presentation to help achieve the next transition towards your final desired emotional state. In the 'Example' above, these elements might be as follows:

▌ **From 'Cynical' to 'Open to Listen'.** You might use pacing to show empathy for how the audience might be feeling now before asking some questions to encourage them to think about the current process from a customer value standpoint to elicit what might be missing now from the process and how it might negatively impact the customer experience in the long term. Alternatively, after showing empathy you might give some facts about the business reality and how the initiative is linked to a desire to improve competitiveness.

▌ **From 'Open to Listen' to 'Curious'.** Now they are 'Open to Listen' you might provide some interesting facts that pique their curiosity, or you might give some information about how world-leading organisations are working to enhance a customer experience and the results they are achieving. Note that these facts would not resonate if given too early – you needed to move them from 'cynical' to 'open to listen' first.

▌ **From 'Curious' to 'Engaged'.** Now the audience is curious, you could set an exercise that engaged them in group discussions about the benefits of having additional customer information and investing more time in the conversations they have. If the group come up with this thinking themselves it is more powerful and engaging than simply being told why it is beneficial.

▌ **From 'Engaged' to 'Motivated'.** Once they are engaged you might start looking at 'what if' scenarios and get them thinking about what commitments they will make to maximise the success of the new process.

Whilst you will need to look at the specific needs of your own presentations to define a) the start and end state for your audience, b) the steps you need to cover on the journey towards achieving your desired end state and c) the elements that you can include in your structure to help you achieve each transition, you can see that this kind of structure focuses on the important thing: how your audience feels.

SUMMARY

▌ Presentations that lack structure often appear rambling, unfocused and disorganised.

▌ Organising and structuring information aids clarity for the audience and improves recall of the information.

▌ Following five key principles will improve the structure and the impact of any presentation.

▌ Have a compelling message: be clear on the objective for your presentation and make the message to your audience more compelling by talking about benefits (rather than features or facts) and using power words like 'improve', 'save', 'solve', 'increase' and 'reduce'.

▌ Utilise the 'Power of 3' to make your key messages more memorable and impactful. Have three key messages where possible or utilise three key words to sum up the message or intention behind your presentation.

▌ Reduce your content: 'less is more'. Most presenters try to put too much content in their presentations. Always keep in mind what you want to achieve and what your audience needs in order for you to achieve your goal.

▌ When you have a lot of information to impart during a presentation, group the information into chunks using the $7^+/^-2$ rule: people find it easier to recall larger amounts of information if that information is grouped so that each group has between five and nine items within it.

▌ Plan your presentation to appeal to emotion not just logic. People buy emotionally and justify logically so you must consider how they might feel about your proposition at the start of your presentation and how you want them to feel at the end if you are to maximise the chance of achieving your outcome. You can then plan steps to achieving this transition in emotion.

8
A high-level structure for all presentations

When planning a presentation it is easy to focus on the detail – the content – at the expense of keeping the big picture in mind. But the 'big-picture' structure is critical in ensuring that your presentation achieves your objectives.

> The 'big-picture' structure is critical in ensuring that your presentation achieves your objectives.

Whenever you present, having a high-level structure that underpins the content you deliver has a number of benefits both for you and for your audience.

A high-level structure helps:

- engage your audience effectively at the start of the presentation;
- ensure that your message is presented clearly;
- maximise the impact of your presentation;
- ensure that you finish your presentation in a positive way;

▌ increase the chance of your audience recalling the
information you deliver.

Many factors can influence your choice of structure, but the
most important consideration is your presentation's purpose
or goal. You need to identify what you want to achieve – do
you want to inspire, motivate, inform, persuade or entertain
people?

Your audience's needs also affect the structure you
choose. For example, those who are new to your topic
need more background information than people with more
expertise and experience. So, in this case, you'd want to
choose an approach that gives you ample time to explain
the context of your subject, as well as to reinforce your
main points.

While each presentation that you give is likely to be
different and so should be prepared for individually
based on your objectives and the audience's needs, there
are a few key chronological elements that are likely to be
relevant to all. We provide below a template that can be
used in most presentations to ensure that you consider
and cover the most important high-level elements. You
can use this standard structure as a rule of thumb,
especially when you are called on to present at short
notice.

You may well have heard of the axiom 'tell them what
you are going to tell them, tell them, tell them what you
have told them' in the context of presenting. While
possibly not as relevant with more senior audiences
(where this structure might bore or frustrate them) it holds
true for a lot of the presentations that you will need to
deliver.

The template we provide below is based on this structure:

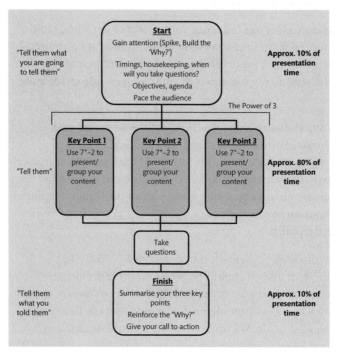

Presentation structure

This structure template incorporates some of the elements of presentation planning that have already been covered in this book and Chapter 9 focuses specifically on creating an impactful start, so we want to focus here on three elements: how you split your time between the start, the middle and the end, taking questions, and the finish.

How to split the time

Our template suggests that the start of your presentation, incorporating all of the components listed, should take approximately 10 per cent of the total presentation time with 80 per cent of the time being spent on delivering the key messages and the final 10 per cent of time devoted to the finish.

Why have we suggested these figures?

The start

Often, presenters dive into their content too quickly, running the risk of either leaving behind or not fully engaging their audience. Put yourself in the shoes of an audience member. You would want to know that the presenter understood how you felt about the topic right now (pacing); you would want to understand what the presentation would cover (agenda); how questions would be handled (should you ask a question when you have one or save it until the end?); how long the presentation would last and if there were any breaks; and, importantly, you would need to know why it was important to you (the 'Why?' or 'What's In It For Me?'). Finally, you would need to know what the purpose or objective of the presentation was.

Covering all of these bases requires time, but the result of investing this time is that the audience will be prepared, ready and possibly eager to move into the content. With longer presentations, you are likely to need more time to cover these items.

The middle

It is appropriate that the biggest proportion of your time is spent delivering the content. Our high-level structure shows how you can utilise both the Power of 3 (ideally have no more than three key points that you want to make) and the $7^{+/-}2$ rule to group content together within each of your key points to ensure it aids subsequent recall. With longer presentations make sure you signpost to your audience where they are within the presentation at regular intervals.

> With longer presentations make sure you signpost to your audience where they are within the presentation at regular intervals.

The end

The end of your presentation is almost as important as the beginning. People tend to remember the first and last things you say so how you summarise and finish is critical to the impact of your presentation. This, again, requires sufficient time to achieve the desired result.

Taking questions

The diagram shows that questions, if taken at the end of your presentation after the delivery of your content, should be handled *before* the final summary. We believe that this is a critical point. Why is this?

What questions are asked by the audience is something that is not in your control. Let us assume for a moment that you have delivered a compelling presentation but find yourself asked a question at the end to which you don't have a strong response. If this is the last interaction your audience has with you, how will this leave them feeling about you and the presentation? While we cannot know for sure, we can assume that, at best, the feeling the audience will leave the presentation with is likely to have been impacted negatively in some way. Imagine giving a strong summary then opening the floor to questions and finishing with a less than positive answer to a question or comment from the audience.

By ensuring that you take questions *before* you move to your final summary you avoid this potential pitfall and ensure that, whatever questions are asked or comments are made, you are in control of giving the final summary. This allows you to better manage the emotion with which the audience leaves the presentation.

We cover the topic of answering questions in detail in Chapter 14.

The finish

The finish is almost as important as the start of your presentation as people tend to remember both the first and last things that you say. After you have taken questions it is important to include a number of elements in the finish:

▌ **Summarise your key points:** This is the 'tell them what you told them' element: if you repeat your key points as part of your summary (for a third time as you will have stated them up front and gone into detail on them in the content) your audience are clear on them and are more likely to recall them later.

▌ **Connect with the audience's motivation:** If your objective is to create some action or a mindset change then it is important to connect the audience with the 'What's In It For Me?' from their perspective: they need to understand why this is important to them.

▌ **Give a clear 'call to action':** Be very clear in confirming what you want people to do as a result of your presentation.

Resist any urge to cover the content of your presentation and finish with a simple 'thank you'. You need to make a strong finish that leaves the audience clear on the key messages, why they are important and what you want them to do. Covering these steps is again something that should not be rushed.

SUMMARY

▌ Having a high-level structure has many benefits to you and the audience including bringing clarity, aiding subsequent recall of information and maximising impact.

▌ The axiom of 'tell them what you are going to tell them, tell them, tell them what you have told them' holds true for many presentations.

▌ We suggest you split the time for your presentation as follows: 10 per cent for the start, 80 per cent for the main content and 10 per cent for the finish.

▌ Take questions before you finish with your own summary; this enables you to control how the presentation finishes and the final message and emotion you want the audience to leave with.

▌ Make sure you create a strong finish where you summarise your key points again, connect the audience with the importance of the topic and provide a strong and clear 'call to action'.

Creating impactful starts

There is a very well-researched psychological concept called the 'serial position effect' which great presenters know about and utilise to help make their presentations more memorable and impactful. The two important components of the serial position effect that impact presenters are the primacy and recency effect which explain that, when asked to recall information, people are more likely to recall things said at the beginning and at the end of a presentation than things said in the middle.

> People are more likely to recall things said at the beginning and at the end of a presentation than things said in the middle.

Information is more likely to be stored, and later recalled, from our long-term memory if we have more time to process it and identify what meaning it has for us. This is easier to do at the start of a presentation and, again, at the end when information and relevance to us is often summarised.

The primacy effect means that the start of your presentation is critical as it is more likely to be recalled and because listeners have a chance to consider what meaning the information you are covering has to them and their context.

Focusing on ensuring that the critical first five minutes of your presentation creates the right impact in your audience dramatically increases the chance of achieving your desired outcome.

What should be included in the first five minutes of your presentation? What is it that great presenters cover in those important first minutes that creates positive impact and increases recall?

The important first words: create a 'spike'

Most of us have attended presentations where the presenter opened with a lacklustre welcome to the audience and proceeded to dive straight into the content of the presentation. The result of this will at best have a mixed effect on an audience. Those who are keen on the topic may well still engage but this kind of start runs the risk of leaving many behind. The start is an opportunity to make an immediate positive impression, to grab the attention of the audience and maximise the chance that their attention will focus on you and your content for the whole of the presentation.

We suggest that, in the case of most presentations you will give as a leader, you start with a spike. A spike is a fact, statistic or statement that is designed to get the immediate attention of your audience with something that is relevant and thought provoking to them. A good spike ensures that your audience sits up and pays attention.

> A good spike ensures that your audience sits up and pays attention.

Here are some examples of spikes that we have heard used to great effect:

▌ To a telecoms industry investors' conference in a presentation on 'opportunity':

'Do you realise that 50 per cent of the world's population have neither made nor received a telephone call?'

▌ By us when presenting on the importance of influencing as a key leadership skill:

'A recent study by Qualtrix shows that we spend on average 23 minutes of every hour trying to move, influence or persuade people. How long have you spent thinking about this skill that you are spending nearly half your working day engaged in?'

▌ Barack Obama in his 2009 inaugural address:

'I stand here today humbled by the task before us, grateful for the trust you have bestowed, mindful of the sacrifices borne by our ancestors.'

▌ To an audience of potential corporate sponsors of a charity by the director of the charity:

'80 per cent of the world's resources are used by 20 per cent of the world's population. There is plenty to go around. The problem is unfair distribution and we are the only charity who can change this.'

▌ At a presentation to underprivileged young people by Dame Anita Roddick, British businesswoman and founder of the Body Shop:

'If you think you're too small to make an impact, try going to bed with a mosquito.'

The ideal spike makes a point that is surprising or interesting or both about the core topic on which you are presenting. Making the spike the very first thing that you say when you stand up to present creates a very powerful impact.

> Making the spike the very first thing that you say when you stand up to present creates a very powerful impact.

Create and build a compelling 'What's In It For Me?'

Most of the presentations that you will deliver will, at their heart, have an outcome that requires some sort of action being taken by the audience. If you think about your own response to requests for action you will appreciate that there are a number of things that contribute to whether you will take the requested action or not. These might include how you feel about the person asking; the specific action you have been requested to take and whether it fits with what you feel to be appropriate and reasonable; the context in which the request is made; and certain other things you need to consider, such as the available time you have or your existing workload.

Another consideration that impacts on whether or not we will take the requested action is whether we can see a compelling personal or group benefit in following through with it. In a lot of cases, even in situations where we might have authority to instruct or demand people to take action, individuals exercise a choice to act based on seeing a 'What's In It For Me?' (WIIFM) benefit. This does not have to be a selfish expression of benefit to the individual. We all take action in service of things other than just ourselves but we do consider the benefits of acting as requested.

Benefits can fall into one of two categories:

▌ something that takes us *towards* something that we want or see benefit in having (outcome achievement); or

▌ something that takes us *away from* something that we want
to avoid (problem avoidance).

Most untrained presenters move too quickly into the 'what?'
of their presentation, the information or content, and do not
spend enough time building the 'why? to ensure that the
audience is ready to listen. Unless the audience is connected
with why this presentation and the suggested or required
action is important and relevant to them, they will not be
fully engaged with the content that you present.

> ▌ **Most untrained presenters move too
> quickly into the 'what?' of their
> presentation ... and do not spend
> enough time building the 'why?'**

To articulate a compelling WIIFM you should do the following:

▌ Put yourself in the shoes of the audience and think about
the *benefits to them* of listening and taking action.

▌ Articulate the positive personal (or group) benefits of engaging
with the required change *and* the negative consequences that
will be avoided by engaging with the required change.

▌ Take enough time to ensure that the WIIFM has been
clearly articulated and understood by the audience.

▌ If possible, use questions to encourage the audience to
think about and connect with the WIIFM: asking questions
promotes thought and increases the sense of responsibility
and ownership that a person feels.

Essential housekeeping

When an audience sits down to listen to a presentation there
will be a number of things that will be on their mind. It is
good practice to cover the most important things as part of
your introduction to the presentation. This has the impact of

enabling the audience to settle much quicker as it signposts expectations and brings them greater clarity.

We suggest that there are three 'housekeeping' items that should be covered in this part of the introduction:

▌ **Timings.** How long will the presentation last? Will there be a break? These simple questions need to be addressed in your introduction. Signposting timings sets the right level of expectation with your audience.

▌ **Handling questions.** How will you handle questions and what is the level of interaction that you would like from your audience during the presentation. With regard to questions there are broadly two options and it is helpful to signpost your preference during the introduction:

▌ handle questions as and when they arise; or

▌ handle questions at an appointed time, often towards the end of the presentation (but in advance of your final summary).

Your choice of option will depend on your personal preference, the topic being covered, the general feeling of the audience towards the topic and other aspects of the context.

A wider question of your expectation around audience interaction can also be covered at this point. You might, for example, want to encourage discussion and contribution in which case you should signpost this in the introduction. Conversely, if you feel you might have a lively audience with lots of views you might want to signpost how you would like to handle contributions. Whatever your decision the point is the same: signpost your expectations so the audience is clear from the start.

▌ **Objectives.** While not strictly in the category of 'housekeeping', one area where your audience will want clarity at the start of your presentation is around your specific objectives for the presentation: what you want to achieve through it. We looked at objectives in detail in Chapter 5. Make sure you are able to clearly articulate what you want your audience to know and be able to do or commit to at the end of your presentation. Signposting this enables your audience to have the necessary context to process and make sense of your content.

Credentialise yourself

In many presentations that you deliver, you will be known by your audience. They will already know the credentials you have that are relevant to you presenting around the topic. It may be that you have authority through your leadership position or through your own personal experience or expertise around the topic.

But there will be times when you are presenting to an audience who, in all or in part, do not have this knowledge or experience of you. In these cases it is important to answer for the audience the question 'What gives you the right to present to me around this topic?' For a number of people, until you answer this question you will not have earned the right to their attention and there is a possibility that they will switch off and not fully engage with what you are saying.

> 'What gives you the right to present to me around this topic?'

Credentialising appropriately requires you to put yourself in the shoes of the audience and think about what they would need to hear to feel that you are credible to be presenting on the topic. It might be that you can tell a story about a similar experience you have had or what you have done in your past that is relevant to the topic you are presenting on.

While this aspect of the introduction may only take 30–45 seconds it is important to have something compelling that answers the 'Why me?' question.

Pace the audience

Chapter 6 introduces the concept of pacing and how to pace an audience effectively. Pacing is the act of acknowledging where your audience might be at the start of the presentation (how they might be feeling about your topic, what their current reality is, etc.). It is critical to include pacing in the introduction in order to a) demonstrate an understanding of the audience's reality and b) earn the right to lead them forward through the presentation towards how you want them to feel about the topic at the end.

> It is critical to include pacing in the introduction.

Depending on the topic, the strength of feeling your audience has about it and the size of any gap that exists between where they are now compared to where you want them to be at the end of your presentation, your pacing might need to be adjusted accordingly. Pacing might be as simple as making a few statements with which the audience can easily agree or it might be that the audience feels more strongly about your topic so that your pacing needs to take longer and possibly enables them to share their views before you can move on. Whichever option you feel is appropriate, ensure that you take enough time to pace the group before you attempt to lead them, or you run the risk of leaving them behind and not influencing them through your content.

SUMMARY

▌ People remember the first things you say so it is critical to create an impactful start to your presentation.

▌ Start with a spike to gain the immediate attention of the audience. This can be a fact, a question or a statement that compels attention and interest.

▌ Make sure you spend time on building the 'What's In It For Me?' for your audience: people buy into an idea emotionally first and then justify it logically. Pay attention to this and do not dive straight into the content before the audience know why it is of benefit to them!

▌ Cover off the essential housekeeping at the start so that the audience can focus on the content. Signpost the timings, breaks, expectations around when you will take questions, how you want the audience to interact with you and each other, and summarise the objectives of the session.

▌ For audiences who do not know you and for those who do but don't know what experience you have in the topic you are to present on, be sure to credentialise yourself: answer the unsaid question 'What gives you the right to present on this topic to this audience?'

▌ Finally, ensure that you pace the audience before you start delivering your content. Remember that they need to feel that you understand how they might be feeling about the topic before you try to influence them to feel something different. Demonstrate empathy through making some statements at the start which acknowledge what their current reality might be.

10

When your presentation is designed to change minds...

In a lot of your presentation situations as a leader a key aspect of what you are trying to achieve through your presentations is to change minds. You might want to introduce a new way of working to your team, sell a new strategy to the company's leadership or to external investors, seek investment in a new idea or win business from new or existing clients. In each of these topics, and in many others that you will face, changing the minds of your audience is often a primary goal.

While some people are open to change, many more are resistant to the idea and feel less comfortable with change. What can you do in your presentations to manage and address this? How can you help people engage with the changes that you are proposing through the medium of your presentation?

This chapter will look first at how people typically respond and react to significant change before covering some priorities for you to focus on if your presentation is seeking to change minds and behaviours.

Natural reactions to change – the Kübler-Ross change curve

Back in 1969 Swiss psychologist Elisabeth Kübler-Ross presented a five-step model in her book *On Death and Dying* that articulated the five stages of grief. You might be forgiven at this point for asking what death and dying has got to do with presenting and why a model used to describe the stages of grief is relevant in a chapter that looks at managing and leading change, so let us explain.

The work of Kübler-Ross has been applied to many aspects of how individuals relate to significant change and has been found to be relevant not just in situations where they experience grief. In fact, in many work-based situations where change is present it is likely that you can see the same model being experienced and played out by individuals and departments.

Change that is imposed on us without our will can impact us deeply. Understanding how we and others are impacted by change can help us manage the situation proactively. It also helps us to see that reactions to change are:

▋ not personal even if they are verbalised to us in a personal way;

▋ part of a process – a journey – that individuals are on in order to engage with the change;

▋ something that takes time to navigate and individuals will move through the process at different rates;

▋ not necessarily indications that either we are doing something 'wrong' or that we will not be successful in implementing the change that we want to see.

> Change that is imposed on us without our will can impact us deeply.

Exercise

Think of a time when you were expected to change something significant about how you worked. It might be that this came as the result of receiving some feedback about something you did. How did you react initially to the feedback or the situation? Did that initial reaction remain or did it change over time? If it changed, how did it change? How long did it take you to fully engage with the change that was requested? How do you feel about that situation now?

As you reflected on that exercise it is likely that you were aware of different stages that you went through in your reaction to a request to change. The Kübler-Ross model articulates these stages:

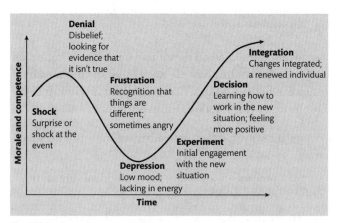

The Kübler-Ross change curve
Source: Reprinted with the permission of Scribner, a division of Simon & Schuster, Inc. from *On Death and Dying* by Dr Elisabeth Kübler-Ross. Copyright © 1969 by Elisabeth Kübler-Ross; copyright renewed © 1997 by Elisabeth Kübler-Ross. All rights reserved.

Change is often uncomfortable for people. Something that you may be feeling very positive about and engaged with can elicit very different reactions in your people if they see it as 'change', and the Kübler-Ross change curve can provide a number of important and useful insights to equip us with awareness about what to expect and how best to handle it.

In the context of your presentations, the curve helps us see that:

▌ Individuals transition through many stages when presented with change.

▌ The initial reaction to change is not necessarily the final reaction – gaining comfort with change can take time.

▌ You may get an initial negative reaction but this is natural in many circumstances and does not represent a failing on your part.

▌ We must not underestimate the feelings that individuals experience around change.

▌ People will require different types of support at different stages of the change curve and we need to be open to providing it.

In many circumstances where we are presenting on something that represents a significant change it would be unreasonable to expect people to not have to transition the stages of the Kübler-Ross curve. We need to recognise this and do our best not to prevent each of the less comfortable stages, but support and manage our people through them. Remember, helping people transition the stages is much more likely to help us achieve a positive long-term result than either ignoring or trying to prevent those stages we might find difficult to manage.

> Helping people transition the stages is much more likely to help us achieve a positive long-term result than either ignoring or trying to prevent those stages we might find difficult to manage.

When planning a presentation that introduces the idea of change, be aware of the Kübler-Ross stages and consider whether shock, denial or frustration (or something similar) might feature in the reactions you could expect from some members of your audience. Ask yourself how you can demonstrate true empathy and recognise these feelings. The technique of pacing covered in Chapter 6 looks at this in more detail. Recognise that change is likely to take time and so do not try to push it through without recognising the genuine feelings that your audience might be experiencing and might still experience long after your presentation.

Once you recognise the stages people go through when faced with change you can take proactive steps to navigate this process and create a greater chance of achieving sustainable change. There are a few key things that you can do in planning and delivering your presentation that will help.

What should you address to help create sustainable change through your presentations?

Based on a reality that over 70 per cent of all major transformation efforts fail in organisations, Dr John Kotter developed an eight-step process for leading change which has been widely used by many businesses over the last 40 years. This process focuses on creating a consistent, holistic approach to changing an organisation and engaging the workforce effectively.

In the context of your presentations we propose a simplified four-step process that links with the work of Kotter but focuses on what you can usefully include and cover in the course of an audience-focused presentation. By considering each of the four components you can increase the chance of communicating your message in a way that is more likely to bring about sustainable behaviour change. Your presentation will not be the only route to achieving this but it can play an important part.

Let us look at the four elements:

1. **Have a 'burning platform'.** A burning platform is a compelling reason for change. If you are asking people to change they need to understand why the change is so important. Building the 'Why?' is often something that leaders do not spend enough time doing in a presentation. Failure to present a compelling reason for change is likely to lead to the audience not seeing change as a key priority for them. You may need to signpost to your audience the positive consequences of achieving the change and the negative consequences of not achieving it as part of communicating the burning platform.

2. **Create a clear and shared vision of the future.** Once people see the compelling need or reason for change they need to know where they are headed: what the future will look like after the change has been successfully implemented. If you create a compelling reason for change but do not paint a clear vision of the future after the change you are likely to get initial action but a lack of follow-through as individuals do not clearly see where they are headed. Think about how you can make the desired future state clear and attractive to your audience and help them see their part in creating that future.

3. **Confirm the ability to change.** If you are asking your audience to engage in change, a key question in their mind once they understand the need for change and see how the future could look is 'Am I able to change?' This question might be at the level of skills, behaviours or around how they think and what they believe is possible. Unless the audience feels able to change in the ways that are required you may experience their frustration: they get the need and are engaged with the vision but do not feel able to change. Give thought to what abilities or behaviours are needed to successfully achieve the desired change and whether your people already have the ability or need some help and support in this area.

4. **Provide clear first steps.** If you want your audience to engage in coordinated activities in order to start the process of change towards where you want to be then you have to give some clear first steps. Without giving clarity about these first steps you run the risk of individuals taking different actions in service of the same end goal. This may reduce your chance of success and make progress difficult to assess and manage.

The following diagram summarises the four steps and what may happen if any one of them is missing from your communication.

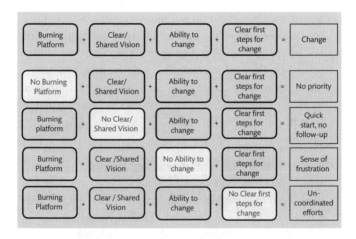

What does all of this mean for your presentations?

Understanding how people may react to significant change and considering some of the key elements of communication that will help secure change should inform how you plan and prepare your presentation. Depending on the type of change you are seeking to bring about and the scale of the change, it may not be realistic to cover everything in a single presentation. Indeed, navigating significant change often takes a lot of time.

> Navigating significant change often takes a lot of time.

There are a few things to bear in mind when your presentations are designed to change minds and actions.

- Pacing the audience is critical – they need to feel that you have real empathy for their reality and situation and also that you understand the discomfort that is often associated with significant change.

- You must make enough time to pace the audience properly rather than come across as being insincere in this.

- Think about the scale of the change and the timescales associated with helping people get comfortable and make the required transition. Resist the urge to try and do too much too quickly as this may well backfire.

- Consider the four elements of change in the diagram above. To what extent have you built a compelling burning platform that your audience can really engage with? Make time to do this early on in a presentation: most presenters rush too quickly to the information (the 'what') and do not pay enough attention to the 'why'. If you do not communicate a compelling 'why' then your audience is unlikely to listen to the detail!

▌ Take time to communicate the future vision: how will things be better after the change has been successfully completed? This might be obvious to you but may not be to the audience. Again, not doing a good job of this means that your audience may not be listening to the detail of your presentation.

▌ Think about what, specifically, you want your audience to do in terms of first steps. Think of this as being similar to building the initial momentum for change to continue. Imagine that your car has broken down and you need to push it off of the road. It takes a bit of energy to get the car moving but once it is moving it is easier to keep it going.

SUMMARY

▌ For a lot of people, change is uncomfortable and so you need to recognise this in your presentations.

▌ The Kübler-Ross curve illustrates the main stages that people go through when faced with significant change and explains that shock, denial and frustration (or variants of these emotions) are entirely normal. Rather than seek to avoid them, look to recognise them and support your people as you help them navigate the change.

▌ When your presentation is seeking to change minds, consider the four elements that are important if you are to achieve a sustainable commitment to change: a burning platform, a clear and shared vision, the ability to change (from the audience's perspective) and the first clear steps for change.

▮ If you do not effectively communicate the burning platform, or reason, for change then your people are unlikely to give it real priority.

▮ If you do not communicate and gain agreement on a clear and shared future vision (how things will be after the change has been successful), then you are likely to get a quick start but no real follow-up.

▮ If you do not create a belief that individuals have the ability to carry out the required change you are likely to feel their frustration.

▮ If you do not give clear first steps and actions then you are likely to get uncoordinated efforts that make it difficult to manage the change.

▮ Recognise that significant change takes time. Resist the urge to try to have your *presentation* achieve too much too quickly.

Part 4

Delivering with maximum impact

11

Performing at your most effective with the C³ Model of Influencing™

How influential are you as a presenter? How can you influence your audiences positively so they get motivated, learn easily, take action and improve their performance when they return to the workplace? The reality is that many of the ways in which we are influenced happen at an unconscious level. One dictionary definition of influencing is: 'producing an effect on an individual or group by imperceptible or intangible means'.

So, what exactly are these 'imperceptible or intangible means'? As a leader, you need to understand consciously what you have to do to get buy-in from as many as possible in any group. You cannot rely on structure, a logical and objective argument or your status in the organisation. More and more nowadays there is a lack of deference to people in authority. You need to earn your right to influence. A useful way of thinking about any presentation is that you are selling both yourself and your ideas to the audience.

> A useful way of thinking about any presentation is that you are selling both yourself and your ideas to the audience.

Exercise

Think of a recent presentation you attended in which you believe the presenter was highly influential. What, in your estimation, was in place for you to make that judgement?

Think of a consumer situation. Remember a time in the last six months when you wanted to buy a product or service – there was no need for you to be convinced. Maybe you were buying a car, a laptop or the latest mobile smartphone. In this instance you decide to buy from a shop, but you leave without buying the product or service because the customer service was poor. Consumer research constantly confirms that if there is dissatisfaction over the level of service people receive when they are thinking of buying a product or service, they will look elsewhere and in many cases be prepared to pay more if they get a much higher level of attentive service. Equally you may have suffered from buyer's remorse when you bought something from a sales person you really liked, but realised afterwards you did not in fact need the product or service. What is going on here?

What happens is that we conflate the person trying to sell us something with the product or service. The two become intertwined. The psychology involved is critical because the same thing happens when you are presenting as a leader. You as the presenter will be conflated in the eyes of the audience with the material that is being delivered. If the material has been structured well and you still deliver it poorly, the design and the material will often count for very little. We will occasionally be prepared to listen to someone presenting to us if their presentation and influencing skills are poor, but usually only when our need is great for the information and/or the presenter is a well-renowned expert.

You cannot not influence: you are doing it all the time when you present. If you are looking to influence more people, more of the time, then there are three elements that need to be in place for you when you present. We call this the C^3 Model of Influencing™.

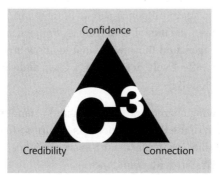

We developed this model when we undertook research for our first book, *Brilliant Selling*, in 2009. This is a book that has sold well over 60,000 copies and been translated into 12 languages. In preparation, we spoke to over 150 top sales people to identify the core skills, behaviours and mindset that allowed them to be top performers. At a high level, we identified three core elements:

1. **Confidence** = your state and your belief in your own ability to influence throughout any presentation.

2. **Credibility** = being believable and having gravitas: comes from your knowledge, your experience and your expertise and also from your body language and voice.

3. **Connection** = that harmonious rapport with the audience that is so vital: you are much more likely to influence positively if the audience likes you.

It is C^3 because it is exponentially more powerful when you have all three elements in place with an audience. If you only have two elements working you will be far less influential. In essence your power to influence revolves around understanding and building these foundations, so you appear naturally charismatic.

We have taught the C^3 Model of Influencing™ to thousands of people who want to influence people in their various roles. We have shared the model with leaders, trainers, sales people, managers and those who want to know how to present more effectively. It's simple to grasp and easy to start using immediately.

In the following chapters we help you understand how to develop each of the three components in turn so that you can ensure that they are in place, with every audience, every time. We will start with confidence.

SUMMARY

- One dictionary definition of influencing is: 'producing an effect on an individual or group by imperceptible or intangible means'.

- You cannot rely on structure, a logical and objective argument or your status in the organisation.

- You cannot not influence: you are doing it all the time when you present.

- The C^3 Model of Influencing™ has three component parts, each of them critical when you present – confidence, credibility and connection.

- It is C^3 because it is exponentially more powerful when you have all three elements in place.

12

How to be confident and charismatic as a presenter

'There are only two types of speakers: those who get nervous and liars.' Mark Twain

Recently we were part of an internal law firm partner conference and a leader stepped up to make a presentation. From the sidelines his behaviour was interesting. As he waited to come on, his confident demeanour from the earlier coffee break appeared to vanish. He walked diffidently to the dais, looked serious and stern and then delivered a bland and unengaging presentation, standing behind a lectern, unsmiling with closed body language. Almost as soon as he completed his presentation, he came off and he slipped back into the confident leader, smiling and chatting with colleagues. What a difference a minute makes! Now of course there is no way of knowing what happened to him before and during his presentation, but he did not exude confidence and this impacted on how his audience perceived and reacted to him. So there was some sort of interference going on. As he was presenting to the group, he did not have the demeanour or gravitas of a leader. He was not 'himself'.

Exercise

If you know confidence is an issue for you, take a moment and think back to a recent presentation you have given. What are the physical manifestations of fear or nerves that you experience? Where does it affect you – your hands, your breathing, in the stomach, restrictions in the neck area, stuttering, shortness of breath?

The great actor and leader Lawrence Olivier would regularly stand backstage, saying of his audience, 'You bastards!', paralysed by stage fright. Stephen Fry left the country for a hideout in Belgium, unable to control the nerves over the opening night of 'Cell Mates'. Paddy Ashdown, an SAS leader and political party leader, wrote in his autobiography that there were times when appearing at PM's Question Time consumed him with terror. Recently, a FTSE 100 CEO we have worked with admitted in a one-to-one session that he avoided delivering presentations as much as possible and attempted to get his number two to deliver whenever feasible, because he lacked confidence when presenting. So, if you know you suffer from nerves or your state is some way from calm and confident, then you are in good company. This chapter is dedicated to providing you, a leader, with practical tips to access a resourceful state at will.

Exercise

What exactly are you frightened of? What makes you nervous? Take a moment and make a list of anything that occurs to you.

Here is a list of some of the most frequent 'frighteners' we have come across in training and one-to-one coaching with leaders:

▌ drying up
▌ looking stupid

▌ being asked a difficult question

▌ being heckled

▌ forgetting key information

▌ the audience turning against you

▌ being boring as a presenter

▌ not articulating a logical argument

▌ the judgement of your peers, your boss or your subordinates.

Most people have some degree of trepidation when speaking in public and very few of us want to look foolish!

Let's start with the basics. Any presentation, whatever the audience and however long or short, is a performance. You can't get away from that. So, just like performing as an actor or musician, you need to find a way to access a resourceful, performance state.

> Just like performing as an actor or musician, you need to find a way to access a resourceful, performance state.

What is a state? A state is your way of being when you are performing a particular task: in this case, presenting. It is a combination of beliefs, emotions, thoughts and physiology. Examples of resourceful states when presenting are calmness, determination and being focused. In contrast, unresourceful states will include fear, anxiety, and feeling unprepared.

Often we think of states only in a negative way – as in 'he's in a right state today' or 'she's got out of bed the wrong way this morning'. During an average day we all go through many different states. We might move from excited, through anxious, bored, happy, curious, confident, and so on. The state you are in when you present is critical and it is surprising how few leaders have developed a routine that works for them to ensure they feel confident and ready to address any group. Many leaders we have spoken to recognise that actually there is little going on in their minds when they are presenting really well. If you are in a positive, confident state when you present you will inevitably be more open, adaptable and able to flex your style. The opposite is clearly true – if you are over-anxious or panicky, it will directly affect your ability to both be and appear confident and assertive and to think on your feet.

In our work with leaders and other people who present on a regular basis, the most desirable state to support an effective and impactful presentation is articulated as 'confidence'. Interestingly, most leaders we work with are already confident in many aspects of what they do. They notice, however, that their confidence can diminish in certain situations and this is often the case when delivering high-stakes presentations. Confidence, therefore, is situational: you can be confident in many aspects of your work and yet lack the necessary confidence in some of the high-stakes situations in which you find yourself.

This chapter looks at how you build the necessary situational confidence that enables you to perform effectively in your high-stakes presentations.

Confidence comes in two forms:

1. **Deep confidence.** An internal confidence born from belief and experience in your abilities and knowledge that you have practised on the edge of discomfort.

2. **Surface confidence.** A confidence that is 'in the moment' and can be created by applying certain tactics and techniques (identified later in this chapter).

Deep confidence

As a leader, there will be multiple situations when you get what you want, you receive the right level of engagement to your ideas, and you communicate easily and elegantly. To be highly effective in an influencing presentation, surface confidence will certainly help but deep confidence is the ideal.

Many top sports people use sports psychologists to help train them mentally to win. The difference, for example, between the top golfer and the 100th best golfer in the world is less than one stroke per round. Their ability level is very similar. So it is all about who can execute the shot at the right time to close out a tournament. That is both about muscle memory and also about the belief the golfer has about his or her ability to win. Even the best can have crushingly disappointing meltdowns. But what separates the great champions is their mindset.

> What separates the great champions is their mindset.

Champion golfer Rory McIlroy famously lost the 2011 Masters after going into the final round with a five-shot lead. He was still leading with eight holes to play but the 21-year-old had a complete meltdown that resulted in a number of shots that were uncomfortable to watch. He ended up scoring 80 and losing by 10 shots, tied for 15th place. Instead of focusing on relevant helpful thoughts (getting ready for each shot), it appeared as though he may have got caught up with the obvious pressure of having the golfing world watch his every stroke (irrelevant thoughts). When athletes stop 'playing to win' and begin 'playing to avoid losing' the result is often increased anxiety, low confidence and poor focus. In McIlroy's case, the fear and self-doubt he started to experience resulted in high anxiety, manifested within the body through muscular tightness, shallow breathing, increased perspiration, rapid heart rate, and butterflies in the stomach. His nerves won. Now, many commentators' immediate reaction was that this experience would be devastating, undermine his confidence and that he would struggle to win a major tournament. However, seeing him interviewed soon afterwards he was more than just sanguine – you could see the desire to put his experience into perspective and move on. He said:

> 'It will be pretty tough for me for the next few days but I will be fine. There are a lot worse things that can happen in your life. Shooting a bad score in the last round of a golf tournament is nothing in comparison to what other people go through.'

Listen to his core beliefs shining through. Just two months later, at the 2011 US Open he won by eight shots. Not a bad way to respond! And now he is a multiple Major winner. Just like the greats of Nicklaus, Ballesteros, Faldo and Player, he retained the right mindset. He understands that his ability to control his mind is critical in his pursuit of further major titles.

The second key element to developing deep confidence is practising on the edge of discomfort. Our last message in all our presentation training events is to go away and practise presenting more often. The more you present, the better you get, as long as you continue to reflect on your performance and get feedback.

Several years ago, we both decided to deliver more conference presentations to large audiences. This is how our Tom and Jerry brand was developed. At the time we could count our large-scale presentations on the fingers of one hand. It took a good year and 20 conference presentations before we were able to feel that sense of deep confidence. Of course, linked to this is rehearsing. When we deliver presentation skills training in our corporate business we are routinely surprised that not all leaders spend enough time rehearsing their presentations. Practice and rehearsal are your best defences against failure. You want to avoid rehearsing in front of a mirror. That is just off-putting and distracting. Ideally you want to rehearse in the same room in which you will present. Ideally, get someone to give you feedback – either a presentation coach or a member of your team. Identify the feedback you are seeking and leave your ego at the door. Rehearsing effectively will hone timings, improve content and improve your sense of deep confidence.

> Practice and rehearsal are your best defences against failure.

Surface confidence

Have you ever engaged in a task when your nerves got the better of you? Most people can look back on some situation, past experience or moment in time when their performance was undermined by nerves – whether it is upper body breathing, constriction in the neck, the voice speeding up or going up an octave. The problem is very simple: if you are not confident when you need to present or influence it will have a double whammy effect. On the one hand, you are focused on yourself rather than the audience, which will impair your performance. And on the other hand, your own lack of confidence will leak out in your body language, voice or the words you use and the audience will pick up on this, usually unconsciously, and start to reject the validity of what you are saying.

Exercise

Take a moment and ask yourself: in an ideal world, what sort of state do you want to be in when you present? Perhaps calm, controlled, empathetic, engaging. Begin with the end in mind.

▶

Now, the key is to direct your nerves in the right way. If you have no nerves at all before an important presentation, then some complacency may have crept in. So it is all about controlling the nerves, the butterflies if you like, and ensuring they fly in formation. What does it take to access this flow, or confident state, when you most need it, in front of a group ready to listen to your message?

The good news is that there are a whole host of techniques, ideas and tools at your disposal that will ensure that when you present as a leader you can be in exactly the state that best suits you. We want to furnish you with as many ideas as possible. The more you can create a strategy that will be effective for you, the more accessing a performance state will become second nature. So take a look at all the ideas we have and test what works for you, out in the real world. These are all ideas that we have taught business leaders and managers around the world to incorporate into their model of preparation.

> The more you can create a strategy that will be effective for you, the more accessing a performance state will become second nature.

Surface confidence tools and techniques to access a resourceful state

Think back on a positive experience

Put yourself in control of your thoughts. Thoughts are one of the elements that impact your state significantly, so choosing your thoughts (rather than being a victim to negative thoughts) is a useful technique to build confidence.

Think of three positive experiences in your life. Now choose the one which has the most resonance. Go back to that time now and remember again what you saw vividly, who was with you, the positive feelings you felt then. Perhaps you are feeling good right now? So here is a simple technique to change how you are feeling in the present and one you can use before any presentation. Your memory will trigger the brain into releasing endorphins which will help you feel great again.

Visualise success

Many of us will have experienced the power of positive visualisation. Jeremy remembers, as a salesman for L'Oreal, being part of a promotion for a new product. The top prize was a new Mini Cooper, and as soon as the promotion was announced he saw himself driving off the stage in the new car. That flicker of the future kept him focused as he strove to win the car and drive off the stage without causing too much of a commotion. Often we do the opposite when confronted with an important presentation. We catastrophise. We imagine the worst – the audience will not like me, I will dry up, I will get a tough question I cannot answer, they will finally 'out' me as incompetent. We have heard the lot.

So do the opposite – visualise a successful outcome. This method is used extensively in sport. Why do Wayne Rooney, Jonny Wilkinson and Andy Murray use visualisation before competing? And could it help you too as a business leader?

Visualise a successful outcome.

Visualisation is proving to be an understandably popular mechanism with elite athletes eager for marginal gains. The use of imagery primes their muscles to perform the correct technique and to execute appropriate actions in competition, but it also conditions their mind to think clearly about how they will react to certain pressures, situations and problems. Consider it a 'mental warm-up'.

On the evening before a Premier League football match, Manchester United striker Wayne Rooney often asks the club's kit man what colour shirts, shorts and socks the team will wear the next day. It's not that Rooney is a closet fashionista eager to match the colour of his boots, underpants or hair transplants to the shades of his team's battle garb. Rooney's mind craves forensic details before a game for one special purpose: to enhance the accuracy of his psychological preparation.

'I lie in bed the night before the game and visualise myself scoring goals or doing well,' he once revealed. 'You're trying to put yourself in that moment and trying to prepare yourself, to have a "memory" before the game.' Knowing exactly which kit he will be wearing helps him conjure up a richer, more detailed and authentic vision. 'I don't know if you'd call it visualising or dreaming, but I've always done it, my whole life.'

For Rooney, this use of imagery – the act of creating and 'rehearsing' a positive mental experience in order to enhance your ability to achieve a successful outcome in real life – is an instinctive method honed since childhood, and one shared by great athletes from Muhammad Ali and Michael Phelps to Jessica Ennis-Hill and Jonny Wilkinson. The late Ali once said: 'I am the greatest. I said that even before I knew I was. I figured that if I said it enough, I would convince the world that I really was the greatest.' And he would often accurately predict when his opponent would be knocked out. Similarly, prior to London 2012, Ennis-Hill revealed: 'I use visualisation to think about the perfect technique. If I can get that perfect image in my head, then hopefully it'll affect my physical performance.'

Likewise, Wilkinson regularly performed visualisation sessions before games: 'You are creating the sights and sounds and smells, the atmosphere, the sensation, and the nerves, right down to the early morning wake-up call and that feeling in your stomach. It helps your body to get used to performing under pressure.'

'The most important thing with imagery is using multiple senses, like sound, sight and smell,' explains sports psychologist Dr Steve Bull, author of *The Game Plan*.

> 'What makes (a player like) Rooney unique is his imagination. When he visualises scoring a goal, he can feel his foot hitting the ball, the smell of the grass under his foot and the sound of the crowd. This incredibly vivid imagery helps an athlete to prepare mentally, by improving their confidence, focus, clarity and speed of thought. It helps them prepare for any scenario: how will I react to the crowd? What if we go 1–0 down? What shot will I take in a certain situation? But it also fires impulses to the muscles, therefore priming them for action. The more vivid the mental image, the more effectively your brain primes your muscles to complete the same physical and technical action in a real game.'

Mental rehearsal can indeed help an athlete to fire up their muscles for optimal performance.

It's not hard to see how these methods from the elite world of sport can be appropriated or adapted for the rest of us in business. Visualisation can galvanise somebody preparing for an important boardroom meeting or a client pitch. 'There is a huge crossover between the demands of sport and business,' concludes Bull. 'For example, if you visualise a big business presentation in real detail, you will prepare for everything from your best posture and body language, and how you will handle any feelings of anxiety, to the awkward questions that might be asked and how you will respond to them. By the time you walk in there, you will feel much more confident.'

In business, as in sport, the more vivid your imagination, the better the results will be. So visualise a successful outcome – your audience applauding, smiling, people coming up and congratulating you, your clients giving you more work. Imagine yourself in your own body delivering a presentation really effectively and then skip to the corner of the room and see yourself present. Do this from as many angles as you like. When you visualise in this way ensure you are seeing yourself in full colour, bright and vibrant, in a movie and as big and panoramic in your mind as possible. Feel your own pleasure at delivering a presentation really well – go on, indulge yourself!

> In business, as in sport, the more vivid your imagination, the better the results will be.

You have 30 minutes until your presentation starts...

Here are a range of suggestions that you can start utilising.

Look up

This is a simple little trick which works to still the mind and avoid the inner voice of doubt taking over. Jeremy was working with a FTSE 100 leader recently and was asking him about his routine before presentations. He talked about spending some time flicking through slides in the few minutes before the presentation was about to begin. When asked what impact this had he admitted that on many occasions this habit ratcheted up the nerves. Doing the opposite works better. In the last 10 minutes or so before you present look up to your right if you are right handed and up to the left if you are left handed. For most people this will mean they become calm and meditative – a useful state in which to present.

Relax

Allow your body to flop down from the waist and as you hang loosely you can totally relax.

Pull up your shoulders to your ears and then relax and release the tension in your neck and shoulders.

Stretch your lips into a silent O and E and repeat ten times.

Yawn – open your mouth as wide as you can. You'll find this relaxes your throat and mouth area.

Breathing

If you are under stress your breathing will naturally become more shallow. Sit back, relax and place one hand on your stomach. Now focus on your natural diaphragmatic breathing – in for a count of five through your nose and then out for a count of ten through your mouth. Repeat this ten times and notice you start feeling calmer.

And if you really understand the value of breathing well, how about the Hawaiian Kahuna 'complete breathing technique'? Native people and infants breathe this way and it can be learned easily. With practice, it can become a habit. Here is how:

1. Stand tall, inhale steadily through the nostrils. Fill the lower part of the lungs first, next fill the middle part of the lungs, finally fill the upper part of the lungs by protruding the upper part of the chest. During this final movement the lower abdomen will be brought in slightly. The inhalation is in fact continuous, even and fluid.

2. Hold the breath for 10 seconds.

3. Exhale slowly through the mouth, holding the chest in place.

You will now be ready to step into the limelight and deliver a great presentation.

SUMMARY

▌ Most leaders experience a degree of fear or trepidation when faced with delivering a presentation.

▌ There is a performance element to every presentation.

▌ A state is your way of being when you are performing a particular task.

▌ You need to be able to access a positive state when you present because this will impact consciously and unconsciously on your audience.

▌ There are two types of confidence – deep and surface.

▌ Deep confidence stems from a positive mindset and from practising on the edge of discomfort.

▌ Avoid catastrophising about an upcoming presentation. Instead, visualise success and detail in your mind exactly how you will deliver an outstanding presentation, just like many leading sports people including Murray, Wilkinson and Rooney.

▌ Develop a plan that covers what you do for the 30 minutes before a presentation and test to ensure it allows you to be confident every time you present.

13

Developing your credibility as a presenter

There are many firms and organisations in which a core competency for a leader is gravitas. Gravitas is very similar to credibility and, as a leader, it is critical to demonstrate this trait when you present. At the heart of being credible as a leader is having the right knowledge to disseminate to the business audience. Knowledge is at the core of your credibility because demonstrating appropriate knowledge and transferring it in the right way will inevitably form part of your outcome. So you need knowledge of:

▌ the subject matter (technical information or other);

▌ your own organisation;

▌ strategy;

▌ your department;

▌ the market;

▌ the challenges you and the organisation face right now;

▌ the participants;

▌ the outcomes;

▌ how to answer the tough questions.

So knowledge is the basic bedrock that you either have or need to acquire as part of the preparation phase. Let's assume then that you are knowledgeable. What other factors will increase your credibility with the audience?

The start

The way you start a presentation will have a huge impact on your credibility. Participants will make meaning of everything you do at the start – your body language, your sense of confidence, how you interact with the group, and so on. This is covered in more detail in Chapter 9.

The way you introduce yourself

You will introduce yourself in different ways, depending on your audience. We have often noticed that presenters will spend little time on introducing themselves. This is a mistake because participants want to know who you are (if they do not know you already) and why you are there. Tell them:

▌ who you are;

▌ why you are the right person to deliver this session;

▌ what you have done in preparation and how you have done the research/analysis;

▌ how your experience will help the group;

▌ something about your life outside work – this helps with connection (see Chapter 14).

Appearance

Whether we like it or not, we will be judged by some on our appearance. Check to make sure you look as good as you can, and match the expectations of the audience. If they are in casual clothes, avoid wearing a suit.

Body language

Our body language when we are presenting will have a direct impact on the way our messages are communicated and accepted by any audience. Bodily communication is any communication without words. It is anything a presenter does to which an audience member assigns meaning. We send and leak nonverbal signals, which may or may not be picked up by the people we are attempting to influence. Nonverbal messages are used to reinforce, replace and unfortunately can occasionally contradict a verbal message. The key thing here is that we have complete control over what we do with our body, and yet we can fall into patterns of behaviour that can reduce or diminish our personal impact. So:

▌ What are the key elements we need to focus on to get our message across in the right way?

▌ What mistakes can we avoid easily and effortlessly?

We think the most helpful way we can direct you here is to offer practical advice as to how best to align your body language with the communication you are intending. Being aware of your mannerisms and unconscious gestures will enable you to bond with and present a confident image to any audience.

> Our body language when we are presenting will have a direct impact on the way our messages are communicated and accepted by any audience.

Sitting or standing?

Should you sit or stand when you present as a leader? We get asked this a lot when we train leaders and of course most people are more comfortable sitting down. Your decision to sit or stand sends a nonverbal signal about your intention to establish authority and power or intimacy and connection. We suggest sitting if it is a small group, an informal presentation, a board meeting, or one in which you need to establish a real connection or deepen a relationship, or if the presentation is very brief and really a precursor to a discussion. You might also, of course, sit during some of the presentation if you want to encourage discussion in the group.

Of course, the real reason many leaders prefer to sit down is that it feels like more of a conversation and there aren't the attendant nerves associated with a more formal presentation. Think about what you're giving up when you sit. Authority is naturally taken by the person standing in a room full of seated people. If you sit down, you give up the authority and let other people take it or at least share it. The result is that it's much harder for a speaker to hold the floor if he or she is seated during the presentation. In most formal presentations, therefore, we would encourage you to stand up to present, even if that means you are out of your comfort zone.

Some leaders use a lectern when presenting. There will be occasions when this is entirely appropriate – for example, formal media events or large conferences when there are lighting issues on the stage. For most other occasions we recommend that you do not use a lectern. This is because it can act as a barrier between you and the audience. It is much better to move and create a closer connection with the audience.

> In most formal presentations ... stand up to present, even if that means you are out of your comfort zone.

Standing position

When you do stand up, ensure you can be seen by all the audience members and avoid at all costs getting in the way of the projector, which will create a shadow.

Undirected movement of the legs and feet suggests nerves and discomfort in front of the audience. We have seen many positions presenters take up when they start presenting including:

▌ one foot in front of the other: this is the tethered animal position – moving towards and then away from the audience in a rhythmic motion;

▌ one foot placed over the other foot making the body appear smaller;

▌ flexing at the knees;

▌ feet too close together;

▌ hopping from one foot to the other;

▌ going on undirected walkabouts;

▌ rising up on to toes.

We have even had one person in our training who started presenting, stork like, with only one foot on the ground!

At the beginning of the presentation make sure you are properly grounded. This means your feet are shoulder-width apart and pointing to the audience. Imagine roots growing into the earth from your feet. You will feel solid and authoritative if you take up this position. How you hold yourself physically is how you hold yourself mentally: so stand tall, avoid slouching and you will be perceived as a confident and authoritative person.

> ▌ How you hold yourself physically is how
> ▌ you hold yourself mentally.

Some presenters like to walk around a lot. Some of you may remember lecturers at university walking up and down across the front of the auditorium. This can get quite mesmeric and can reduce impact. We remember one trainer who used to walk into the audience regularly and that was effective at keeping attention and interest. It is also possible to use the space in front of the audience in a very directed way to emphasise certain points. This is called stage anchoring. It is a useful technique to employ if, for example, you want to talk about what has happened in the past, present and future. You simply talk from different positions and this can be dynamic and memorable. Visit our website (www.theleadersguidetopresenting.com) to access a video that demonstrates how stage anchoring can be used.

Eye contact

The eyes have it! There is that old expression that your eyes are the gateways to your soul. We express our emotion through our eyes. Certainly eye contact is critical to reinforce your connection to any audience.

Subconsciously you may not want to be standing, exposed and ready to have judgement passed upon you, and you may avert your eyes, as you do on a crowded Tube train, in lifts or walking along a street late at night, because if you don't look you don't communicate. However, as a speaker you need to communicate with your eyes, not like a scared rabbit that has to check all the escape routes, but in a calm and interested manner as you would when talking to a good friend.

Avoid looking at:

▌ visual aids;

▌ the floor or ceiling;

▌ your notes;

▌ the most senior person present;

▌ the friendliest person present;

▌ or even out of the window.

People who do not offer eye contact in general conversation are sometimes seen as shifty or nervous. Looking at your listeners demonstrates that you are interested in them and helps them to concentrate on what you are saying because they will feel you care about their reactions. Looking at your listeners helps you to see them as individuals and relate and respond to them. In addition, powerful people give more eye contact than those who are less confident.

> Looking at your listeners demonstrates that you are interested in them and helps them to concentrate on what you are saying because they will feel you care about their reactions.

You will want to avoid skimming the audience by looking at them too fleetingly. Equally it is not good to focus too long on someone. Some trainers suggest finding a friendly face in the crowd and focusing on one individual. This is poor advice. The way to play it initially when you start speaking is to *look at as many of the audience members as possible for the amount of time it takes to say 'elephant, elephant'* – just a few seconds will do it. Sounds ridiculous but you may just remember it!

Facial expression

Too often we notice when we work with leaders on improving their presentation skills that they look very serious and severe. This is usually because they are in a state that is not ideally supportive of presenting effectively. They may be anxious, nervous or unsure. So the best thing to do is smile and look as though you are enjoying what you are doing. Some presentations may require you to be quite serious but most will lend themselves to you looking and sounding as though you want to be there. What is your 'I am happy' expression?

If you feel intimidated by your audience, then this will show through. Jeremy remembers a time when he had to present to the board and he did not handle this well. He then read somewhere that one way to think differently about the audience is to think of them with Donald Duck hats on or sitting on the toilet. Either way, the next time he presented to this group he was able to smile easily.

If you smile there is a good chance many audience members will smile back at you. It will relax you as well – you will be using around 26 muscles in your face.

> If you smile there is a good chance many audience members will smile back at you.

Hands

The resting position is the position of your hands when you first start presenting and the one you return to when you are not overtly using gestures.

What not to do with your hands:

- **Hands in pockets.** This can be interpreted as far too casual and may suggest that you are not entirely serious. This can reduce your credibility.

- **One hand in a pocket.** This may still appear too casual and looks lop-sided, although is better than two hands in your pockets.

- **Hands behind torso.** Too authoritarian – reminiscent of someone from the police, armed forces or royalty.

- **Prayer position.** Hands entwined together in front of your chest. The impact of this posture is often to make you rigid and tense which may communicate nervousness to your audience.

▌**Hands folded over chest.** The audience may believe you are being defensive, protective and closed and can make you appear more tense to the audience.

▌**Hand on hip.** This looks unbalanced.

▌**Hands over groin area.** This is the footballer's wall position. It looks too protective and closed.

▌**Fiddle.** Avoid fiddling with nails, rings, cuff links, buttons or coins in pockets (remove all coins before the presentation begins!).

All these unconscious gestures are habit patterns that come from nervousness. Finally, it is best to avoid holding anything, unless you have to hold a pointer to move the slides on.

What you are looking for is neutrality in your initial body position because you want the audience to immediately start focusing on what you are saying. There are two neutral positions – one of them is to keep your hands down by your side. The other is to place one hand over another softly around the navel area. It is called a resting position because your hands can start there and return there when you are not gesturing. Either resting position will work effectively – it's just a matter of choice. Try both in your next few presentations and identify what is most comfortable for you.

Gestures

While it is important to take up the resting position (feet shoulder-width apart and arms by side or comfortably on navel) at the beginning and end of the presentation, you will potentially appear wooden if there is little movement from your arms.

Some presenters gesture more than others – it is down to style and habit, as well as culture. When we work in Italy or

South America it is very noticeable that presenters use big gestures more often. But how important are gestures in communicating your message? In recent research into successful TED Talks, an interesting fact emerged: the more hand and arm gestures, the more successful the Talk. There was a direct correlation between the number of views on a TED Talk and the number of hand or full arm gestures.

The bottom TED Talks had an average of 124,000 views and used an average of 272 gestures during the 18-minute Talk. The top TED Talks had an average of 7,360,000 views and used an average of 465 gestures – that's almost double! Why do we think this is? Our hands are a nonverbal way to show and build trust – studies have found that when we see someone's hands, we have an easier time trusting them. Also, when someone uses their hands to explain a concept, we have an easier time understanding them. Speakers who use gestures are speaking to their audience on two levels– verbally and nonverbally. The bottom line appears to be – if you want to be a good speaker, let your arms and hands do the talking.

> The bottom line appears to be – if you want to be a good speaker, let your arms and hands do the talking.

Your gestures should, of course, coincide with what you are saying and naturally add emphasis to your words. Some presenters do not use the whole of their arms when gesturing – they appear to have Velcro elbows! They may just not be as expressive or often are simply more self-conscious or nervous and restrict natural movements because of this. Remember that gestures should include the whole of your arm and not be restricted to small meaningless hand movements.

If you want to appear more credible then one simple way to achieve this is by keeping your palms down when gesturing.

You will notice that many politicians do this when they present. If the palms-down gesture is also accompanied by a dip of the head at the end of a sentence when you are mentioning your key points you will emphasise your credibility even further at an unconscious level.

The converse is also true – if you want to connect with the audience then use palms up. This will naturally invite connection. The palm facing up is used as a submissive, non-threatening gesture, reminiscent of the pleading gesture of a street beggar and, from an evolutionary perspective, shows the person holds no weapons. Use open palms when you are asking questions or when you want to get ideas from the group.

SUMMARY

▌ Knowledge is at the heart of your credibility.

▌ Stand when you present if you want to have the power and authority.

▌ Ensure you are properly grounded when you start to present.

▌ Ensure you have eye contact as soon as possible with the audience members.

▌ Smile – it relaxes you and the audience.

▌ Remember to have a neutral resting position – either with your hands by your side or clasped softly over the navel.

▌ Use big gestures, which all improve your gravitas.

14

Connecting with any audience

As business presenters we need to get on the same wavelength as our participants. Connection is the naturally occurring dance that happens when people meet. Sometimes it happens spontaneously. However, there are specific skills and behaviours you can learn that enhance connection and increase your effectiveness as a communicator and influencer.

Connection (or rapport) is fundamental to effective presenting. Rapport is one of the cornerstones of effective personal impact. If you learn these key skills you can have more control, and influence others unconsciously. When you are in rapport with your audience, the people tend to be more open to you, be less critical, have fewer objections and be more likely to accept what you say.

> Rapport is one of the cornerstones of effective personal impact.

Connection is matching the way you communicate to the way the group takes in information. It increases the likelihood that the message you send will be the one they receive. It promotes trust and comfort in people. So use language that will resonate, jargon if it is common parlance.

People buy people who are like themselves. As a rule we most prefer to say yes to the requests of people we know and like. The liking rule produces assent. So we need to demonstrate that we know the group's world, that we understand their language and the challenges they face in business.

In a business context your communication will have a purpose – you want to influence them, teach them new information or skills, persuade them to change, explain a new strategy or help embed new behaviours or skills.

Here are 10 top tips on building a connection with any audience:

1. Use any contacts you have to understand more about the audience – find out as much as you can about them: their likes, dislikes, their proclivities and the hierarchy within the group.

2. Maintain a total focus on the audience – by being fully absorbed in what is going on for that period of time you have forgotten to even think of other business issues or other things playing on your mind.

3. Shake hands or speak to as many of the audience as possible – this builds an immediate connection and you can get to hear people's names and start using them straight away.

4. Use comprehension questions to test understanding – 'Does that make sense?' 'What is your view?' 'What questions come to mind about the direction we are taking?'

5. Have fun – most people digest or learn more when they are enjoying themselves, so keep it light, even with tricky subjects.

6. Use humour – you do not need to be a joke teller but be open to humour throughout a presentation. It's good to

make your audience smile and this relaxes them naturally. The key thing is to be open to humour and use it appropriately when you get the chance. Self-deprecating humour works best – demonstrate your weaknesses or admit your failings. Humour that works well and creates laughter and positive energy in the room:

▌ demonstrates that the presenter is relaxed and resourceful;

▌ relaxes individuals and may relieve any nerves some may be feeling;

▌ establishes a bond with the group;

▌ maintains interest in the subject and the participants' attention;

▌ can help emphasise a specific point;

▌ can turn an awkward moment into an enjoyable experience;

▌ is an effective tool to increase learning, creativity and retention.

7. Be open about yourself and your personality – divulge snippets about yourself and use your own experience to underpin an idea.

8. Identify common interests – if lots of people in the group are interested in sport or food or travel use lots of stories about these subjects.

9. Remember names – there are plenty of techniques to do this. We tend to use the person's name immediately and also (in our own minds) stick their name cards on their foreheads.

10. Be curious and ask questions – find out what the audience really think, probe when there is obvious interest and tap into the wealth of experience in the room.

Take a moment and think back over the last few months and recall two or three powerful stories that you have heard. As you consider each of these, in what contexts can you apply and use them to support or increase the appeal and impact of a presentation?

Perhaps the most powerful way to connect with any audience as a leader is to tell stories. The ancient art of storytelling can change the way we think, act and feel. It works with all cultures. Leaders, especially, can use the power of a good story to influence and motivate their groups to take action. Stories can be inspirational. They can create legends that an entire workplace culture can build upon, and they have the power to break down barriers and turn a bad situation into a good one. Stories, if you can make them crackle and fizz with electricity, can capture imaginations and make things real in a way that cold, hard facts can never do. We share our stories to inform, enlighten and entertain because they touch the imaginations and emotions of our audiences. Stories can be very, very powerful influencing tools. Great leaders know this, and many top CEOs, politicians and professional communicators today use stories to illustrate points and sell their ideas.

> Perhaps the most powerful way to connect with any audience as a leader is to tell stories.

When we say stories we mean real personal anecdotes, stories you have heard other leaders or presenters use, corporate case studies, metaphors, fables, analogies and research references. They add colour and substance to all business communication. Done really well they can bring any session to life. Why are stories such an integral part of influencing a group? Essentially the power of stories is hardwired into us from birth. We are constantly being told stories – by our parents, grandparents, teachers and friends. Stories are part of the very fabric of what makes us human. They connect us to our past, contain messages that tell us how to live and entertain us. If you are a parent you will know about the magic of telling a bedtime story to a child and will have noticed how a child's face glazes over and becomes entranced almost as soon as you mutter the words 'Once upon a time…'

The best state for any audience is a state of curiosity. Stories elicit this curious state in participants. You can see them relax, sometimes go into a light trance and listen intently to the story, however long or short. If you pepper your presentations with stories it's a sure-fire way to guarantee a high level of curiosity, which will result in your content being accepted easily and effortlessly.

What exactly do we mean by a story? A story is a way of organising information. It will typically have some structure – a beginning, middle and end. It will incorporate a sequence of events, involve people and give the presenter a chance to say what needs to be said without being didactic or overly persuasive. The metaphor of the cloak works well here. The story is a cloak that covers what we want to say in an accessible way, and often allows us access to a deeper meaning.

Of course, stories (especially ones that happened to you) are easy to remember for the leader. However, another great benefit of telling stories is that they create emotion in participants. Stories will create feelings of happiness, sadness, disappointment, optimism and anticipation. The reason why this is so vital is that emotions help create motion. In other words you are more likely to get people motivated to change – one of the underlying purposes of all presentations delivered by leaders. The best stories can result in changes at both a conscious and unconscious level in the listeners. When you appeal to the audience on an emotional level by using a story, they're more likely to remember you and your ideas. Think about some of the great storytellers of the last century – Martin Luther King, Mahatma Gandhi, Nelson Mandela and Winston Churchill for example. They all told stories that inspired the masses to take action.

The following table lists a variety of reasons or points in your presentations when stories may be appropriate:

When to use stories	Why?
At the beginning	Creates curiosity, sets the tone, gets the group thinking, can set up a theme
To clarify facts and data and add evidence to what you are saying	Supports and emphasises the content or theory – it will make complex ideas easier to understand and is much more entertaining
If you need to establish your credibility	A new audience may not yet be convinced you can teach them anything – choose a story that demonstrates you can do what you are teaching
To build a connection with your audience	Demonstrates you can identify your audience and begin to build a rapport – if it comes from personal experience, it will help you gain their empathy and trust and break down barriers

▶

When to use stories	Why?
To be persuasive	People accept ideas more readily when they're presented in story form rather than factual data – for example, storytelling is used prolifically in advertising in an attempt to get you to buy a product or service
To challenge an individual or a group	Sometimes they may be in 'group think' and not be open to new ways of doing things – individuals may be holding on to limiting beliefs that are stopping them moving on
To demonstrate how to do or not to do something	Brings the subject alive and helps convince the audience it is possible – stories help embed best practice, so get participants to share their stories if at all possible
At the end of the presentation	Links to final message and to action back in the workplace

Here are some thoughts on the 'how to' of telling stories. Keep these suggestions in mind when telling stories that bring your presentations alive.

▌ **Pay attention to your audience.** Every presentation should be focused on the audience's needs. Think carefully what will work best for the group that will be in front of you.

▌ **Get to the point.** Draw in your audience with enough detail, but be careful not to drag it out. If you don't keep the story moving and get to the point, you may lose the audience.

▌**Be yourself.** The best storytellers talk from their hearts, so don't try to fake an emotion that you don't feel.

▌**Create a vivid experience.** Dig deep into the reservoir of your vocabulary and show your listeners the picture you're painting, don't just tell them. Try to engage the five senses in every story: taste, touch, sight, hearing and smell. They'll make your story come alive.

▌**Practise.** Rehearse, rehearse, rehearse. It's all about rehearsing to get it in the muscle and then acting spontaneously.

▌**Use a model for storytelling.** Try the story–point–benefit framework. While it is not always necessary to be explicit with your story it can be helpful for some audiences to tell them the *point* of the story and then the *benefit* they will get if they improve the skill or master the new behaviour.

▌**Try nested loops.** This is a common tool used in neuro-linguistic programming (NLP) and hypnotism. It is based around starting but not completing a story until later in the training. Great comedians such as Billy Connolly, Woody Allen, Ronnie Corbett or Jackie Mason do this as part of their routines. A typical nested loop structure starts this way: open story a – story b – story c, – close story c, story b, story a. Basically, if you don't complete your story, you cause an open loop. Ideally, before you close the loop, you embed ideas and suggestions that go into the unconscious. This is great to use when you dealing with change and personal development.

And so here is a story. Like many good stories, this one exists in different versions. Some feature a Poodle, or another small breed of dog instead of a Chihuahua. You could use this to illustrate assertiveness, decision-making under stress, if you want to change beliefs about what is possible, or emphasise creative thinking, quick thinking, bluff or boldness.

A lady takes her pet Chihuahua with her on a safari holiday. Chasing butterflies, the dog wanders too far one day and gets lost in the bush, under a tree. Soon it starts to whimper and the situation is made worse when it encounters a very hungry-looking leopard. The Chihuahua realises he's in trouble, but, noticing some fresh bones on the ground, he settles down to chew on them, with his back to the big cat. As the leopard is about to leap, the Chihuahua smacks his lips and exclaims loudly, 'Boy, that was one delicious leopard. I wonder if there are any more around here.'

The leopard stops mid-stride, and slinks away into the trees.

'Phew,' says the leopard, 'that was close – that evil little dog nearly had me.'

From the tree, a monkey sees everything and thinks he'll win a favour by putting the stupid leopard straight. The Chihuahua sees the monkey go after the leopard, and guesses he might be up to no good.

When the leopard hears the monkey's story he feels angry at being made a fool, and offers the monkey a ride back to see him exact his revenge.

The little dog sees them approaching and fears the worse.

Thinking quickly, the little dog turns his back again, pretends not to notice them, and when the pair are within earshot says aloud, 'Now where's that monkey got to? I sent him ages ago to bring me another leopard...'

How to answer questions from the group

How do you handle questions that get fired at you as a presenter and leader? This is where you will earn your crust. Questions from the audience can make or break both your connection and credibility. Many presenters fear questions and often deliberately avoid taking them. People want answers to personal concerns or challenges and so we need to do everything we can to encourage questions and then answer them effectively.

> Questions from the audience can make or break both your connection and credibility.

A great way to plan any presentation is to ask yourself: 'If I was in the audience's shoes, what questions would I ask?' Then build your session around the answers to these questions. When we are coaching leaders we often ask: what are the top five toughest questions you really don't want to be asked? If you can answer these ones easily through preparing for them, then all other questions will be straightforward and you will feel more comfortable in the presentation knowing you can deal with them if they are asked. The final element in preparing is to decide when and how you are going to take questions – throughout the session or at the end?

The questions you get may be tough and you may not be able to answer them immediately. If you start getting nervous or demonstrate that you are uncomfortable you will undermine your own credibility. So you need to really listen to the question, ensure you continue to diaphragmatically breathe and (literally) keep your head up (see Chapter 12). Smile, retain eye contact and, if you need to, find a way to think before you answer. When you are taking questions at the end, you can give yourself more time to think if you collect all the questions on a flip chart. The other advantage of this method is that it allows you to decide the chronology of the questions. You may decide to leave the one that has the most impact until the end.

Not all questions will be straightforward to answer. You are going to be challenged and it is useful to get a sense of what to do when faced with these challenges. When we train groups we identify from them what the key concerns are about handling questions. Here is a series of common concerns about handling questions. Take these ideas on board and it will allow you to have more flexibility in the way you handle typical questions that crop up on a regular basis when you are presenting as a leader.

'How do I encourage questions if there are none?'

Most of us would like people in the audience to ask questions. A lively Q&A session after your initial presentation is stimulating and engaging for the audience. But sometimes you ask for questions, and you're just met with blank gazes back from your audience. It's a let-down and your presentation potentially ends on a sour note. In order to avoid this happening, here are some suggestions:

▍ Encourage the audience to ask questions throughout the presentation. Tell people they can interrupt you throughout the presentation to ask questions as they come to mind. This has several benefits – people won't have to remember their question till later, if they're uncertain about something they can get that clarified at the time and questions on a particular issue are dealt with at the same time that you're discussing that issue.

▍ Lobby in advance and ensure that there are people willing to ask questions.

▍ Kick start the question period with, 'A question I am often asked is…' Then answer your 'question'. This helps to prime the pump and encourages others to ask questions. Have a few of these rhetorical questions ready, just in case.

▍ At the end of the presentation, say to the audience: 'I suspect many of you will have questions for me right now.

Take a moment, and jot down the three key questions that you have, and then I will attempt to answer these questions in three minutes.'

▌ Alternatively, you could ask them to get into pairs and identify the questions they want to ask. This will pretty much guarantee that you will get some questions.

'What if I don't know the answer to a question?'

It is best to be honest here. Do not try to fake it. If you cannot answer because you do not know, admit it, look confident and tell them what will happen so that the question can be answered at some future date. Avoid the stammering attempt to answer as this will reduce your credibility. Just think about how you can get the answer the person is looking for – this could be done quickly in a break or you may need to ask a colleague or do some additional research. Be sure to follow up and provide the answer in a timely way. The only other alternative is to open the question to the audience if appropriate as it may get you out of a hole.

'How do I handle a question if I believe someone is trying to trip me up?'

This is a tough one. You can't be certain that someone is trying to trip you up. It may be that the person is simply trying to extract some information, and yet it comes across as hostile. So, here are a few options:

▌ Flatter the individual – tell the person it is an interesting question and ask for his or her perspective.

▌ Ask the person for the reason behind asking the question – why is this important to you?

▌ Ask the audience if it is something they would all be interested in –if not, then you can suggest you take it offline and then speak to the person at the break.

'What if I get a statement from an individual, rather than a question?'

Sometimes you will have a listener raise his or her hand and instead of asking a question will make an extended comment – or a speech. This person has no question.

A way to handle this is to watch the person's speaking rate, and when he or she takes a moment for a breath interrupt with 'Thanks for your comment... Is there a question linked to it?' You may have to look at another part of the room and encourage questions from the others. Do not allow the person to continue with the 'speech' because it will deprive other members of the audience of the opportunity to ask questions.

'What if the question is not relevant?'

In this case, you may have to be directive and move quickly to another question. You can also suggest you take the question offline. You could, alternatively, ask the questioner to rephrase the question or ask the person why he or she thinks it is important.

'What if I get a question which I have already answered?'

Even if it is tempting, you will want to avoid patronising the questioner, by saying that you have already covered this. Acknowledge and confirm the nature of the question and then answer it directly. It gives you an opportunity to press home one of the key themes of the presentation.

'What if I get a politically sensitive question?'

Occasionally, questions will fall outside of the remit of your presentation or you feel you cannot answer a question because it is politically sensitive. If the latter, then you must be assertive and upfront about this and explain why, at this stage, it is not possible to divulge the answer and move swiftly to the next question. Resist taking sides or positioning yourselves on the 'side' of the participant.

The 4 A Model

So, what is a useful step-by-step guide to answering questions in any presentation?

Here is the process we teach presenters to use when answering questions: the 4 A Model. It can be used whenever you get a question from an individual or from a small group.

▌ Acknowledge

▌ Audience

▌ Answer

▌ Ask

Here is a little more detail on each step.

Acknowledge

Remain silent, listen carefully and ensure that you understand the question. Treat all questions equally and without judgement. Acknowledge the individual who has asked the question. This may be a simple 'thanks for that question, John'. However, you may need to ask the person to rephrase it if it appears convoluted or comes out as a statement, and to a large audience we recommend you repeat the question. Some may not have heard the question.

Audience

If appropriate, allow the questioner or someone from the audience to answer the question. This gives you time to think and it may well be that an audience member can answer it perfectly well. This works less well with large groups. You might say 'That's an interesting question, what do you think?'

Answer

Avoid a long diatribe and if you have already covered the question avoid the sarcastic 'well we looked at that an hour ago' response. Maybe you weren't clear enough and further explanation is required. We do not recommend the bridging technique so beloved of politicians when they are answering questions from journalists. For example:

> 'That's an interesting issue but what the public are most concerned about is...' or 'Some say that and what our research shows is...'

The public is fed up with this approach and it tends to undermine trust in politicians. It's best to answer the question head on. Keep to a maximum of three points and spend a maximum of two minutes answering. If you can be certain of the answer and the questioner is looking for certainty, then provide certainty. However, in some cases you will position your answer as just one option and seek ideas from the rest of the group after you have spoken. As the leader, you do not necessarily have a monopoly on the truth.

Ask

Go back to the person who has asked the question and check that the question has been answered satisfactorily. A simple 'Does that answer your question?' will suffice. Be sure to respond if they answer negatively. If someone answers your question with a 'Not really' then you need to probe to find out what else they might need and start the process from

'Acknowledge'. Not doing this can undermine credibility and trust.

Embedded commands

Finally, especially if your presentation is intended to change people's perceptions, be persuasive or motivational then you can easily use 'embedded commands'. An embedded command is a series of words that are embedded within a sentence which commands the audience to do something. You are giving the command wrapped up or embedded in a longer sentence. Using embedded commands is incredibly powerful because you will be influencing people at an unconscious level. They are often used in sales and marketing. You can use them when you present by putting emphasis on what you want the audience to do. Here are some examples:

> 'You, **like me**, are invested in making this work.' [The embedded command here is **like me**.]

> 'If you are sure right now that **you want to use us for this project**, then...'

> 'How many of you sitting here today know that **change is inevitable** if we want to achieve our goals?'

SUMMARY

▍ Connection (or rapport) is one of the cornerstones of effective personal impact.

▍ The audience want to connect with you – do this through shaking hands at the outset, questions, humour, being open, having fun and through variety in delivery.

▌ Breathe deeply to ensure your voice is at its best.

▌ Tell stories – you have a reservoir of them to draw on.

▌ Ask yourself at the preparation stage: what are the five worst questions I really don't want to be asked?

▌ Use the 4 A Model to answer questions – Acknowledge, Audience, Answer, Ask.

▌ The best presenters find a myriad of ways to use embedded commands when they want to influence others at an unconscious level.

How to be credible and connect using your voice

Exercise

Take a moment to record your voice and then play it back. As you listen to the recording, what, specifically, do you notice about your voice: its tone, volume, pace, etc.? Try to be objective – what works and what would you like to change in your voice?

Not many of us like the sound of our own voices. Indeed, when we train leaders it is very rare that leaders like the sound of their own voice when they hear themselves on a video playback. To be an effective speaker you need to be heard, to be understood and to have variety in your voice. Your voice is a critical tool that underpins your effectiveness as a speaker.

The secret of effective voice projection is to breathe from your diaphragm. If you breathe deeply then you will not have to use as many throat muscles. The deeper you breathe, the more breath you will have to sustain your voice and project it to listeners. So what are the key elements that will allow your voice to be heard as a presenter?

▌ Use variety in speed, volume and pitch.

▌ You will need to speak louder than normal (unless you are miked up). This does not mean shouting obviously, just up your volume by around 10–20 per cent. You need to aim for communication without intimidation.

▌ If you naturally have a fast delivery, you will need to slow down.

Pausing is one of the most overlooked delivery techniques, but there are many benefits of using pauses effectively. Pauses allow you to:

▌ slow your rate to match the audience's listening capacity;

▌ convey emotion;

▌ take a breathe;

▌ really engage the audience;

▌ catch up with your mind.

Pauses can really emphasise certain key points that you wish to make, especially if you pause just before and/or just after making the point itself. Pause for a little longer than you might usually – perhaps for two or three seconds. The impact of the pause is further enhanced by freezing your body at the point you start the pause and not moving it again until you start speaking. The key is that your verbal pause is in sync with you ceasing to move your body.

> ▌ Pausing is one of the most overlooked delivery techniques, but there are many benefits of using pauses effectively.

For example:

> 'We are reaching a critical time for the business (pause). In order to hit our five-year target (pause), we all need to

be aware of the changes necessary to be successful (pause). We can do this (pause) if we all pull together now.'

Other tips include:

▌ Avoid ums and ers or filler words such as 'you know', 'I mean', 'basically'.

▌ If you want to add colour to your voice, emphasise certain words or phrases that are most important for messaging.

▌ Ensure your voice has a higher-level intensity than a mere conversational voice. To do this effectively you need to show emotion and energy in your voice to ensure your key messages really land.

▌ Have a drink of water available – you can use this to help a dry mouth and for a dramatic pause.

We have seen that both credibility and connection are two of the vital components of influencing when presenting. Both can be established and enhanced by how you use your voice. We found a really useful analogy in a great little book called *Charisma – The Art of Relationships* by Michael Grinder.

When you get on an aeroplane often the first person you will hear is the captain (90 per cent of captains are male) as in 'Welcome aboard, my name is Captain Cassell. We will be pushing back in approximately 20 minutes and…' At some point you will also hear the voice of a flight attendant: 'We have a great crew with us today – Bob and Angie will be coming among you shortly…'

Now, have you ever noticed that often they talk in very different ways? Next time you are on a plane you may well notice the following differences in their voices:

Captain – vocal qualities	Flight attendant – vocal qualities
Slow	Fast
Intonation goes down at the end of the sentence (often visually accompanied by a small head dip at the end as well)	Intonation often goes up at the end of the sentence or phrase
Uses pauses	Uses few if any pauses
Short, clipped sentences	Long, possibly rambling sentences
More monotone	Lots of variety and musicality in the voice
Focus on facts and objective information	Focus on people-orientated information

Essentially, the captain uses a 'credible' voice pattern. This is entirely understandable as we are generally not that interested in the captain's ability to connect. In fact, it is a little disconcerting when the captain tries humour. It seems rather incongruous. We want him to know everything about the control panel in front of him and focus on getting us to our destination in one piece. The flight attendant uses a 'connection' voice pattern which is entirely in keeping with crews' role on board – to put their customers at ease, sell to them and offer great service so they stay loyal to the airline.

Barack Obama and David Attenborough are examples of the credible voice and Jamie Oliver and Dawn French are good examples of the connection voice. Go to our website to hear more examples of the credible and connection voice patterns – www.c-cubedinfluence.com. How do we suggest applying these ideas to your presenting?

▌ Use both voice patterns throughout your presentation and think carefully about which voice pattern will fit most easily with your intention.

▌ Use the credible voice pattern when you are trying to be authoritative, when you are lecturing or wanting to emphasise key points.

▌ Use the connection voice pattern when you want to put people at ease and demonstrate that you are interested in them as people.

Here is a quick practical guide to give you a sense of when each voice pattern is appropriate:

Situation	Use credible voice pattern	Use connection voice pattern
Meeting people for the first time		✓
The start of any presentation	✓	
Teaching theory or knowledge	✓	
Answering a question	✓	✓
Facilitating a debrief	✓	
Talking to people during breaks		✓
When you want them to take action	✓	
Giving feedback	✓	✓
Using humour		✓

SUMMARY

▌ Vocal variety in speed, volume and pitch is critical to keeping your audience engaged.

▌ Healthy diaphragmatic breathing is central to a good voice – do breathing exercises before delivering.

▌ You can build your credibility and connection by using variety in your voice.

Part
5

Specific high-impact presentation situations for leaders

The following four chapters look in more detail at some specific high-stakes presenting situations and provide some practical tips to aid your planning, preparation and delivery.

16

Pitching for success

As a leader, you may never be part of a pitch. You may have managed to delegate! Many leaders are, however, an intrinsic part of the pitching process in order to win work. Sales pitches can be formal or informal, in front of few or many, take a few minutes or several hours, and the leader may play a variety of roles. We are dealing here with the formal pitch – perhaps an hour or so, with questions at the end. There is a lot riding on a pitch and so clearly this is one of the most important high-stakes presentations. Often a huge effort is required in time and energy in order to deliver a really effective pitch. So the first fundamental question to ask yourself and your team is a simple one – is this really worth it? You need as a team to decide consciously about whether to pitch. If you do get involved, you will have no authority over the audience, and you will be part of a pitch team in which you may not be leading. So this type of presentation will require you to be flexible, use all your influencing skills, and identify and then communicate why you are involved.

Questions to ask yourself

Derek Klyhn, a partner at our Møller PSF business, carried out research into buyers of professional services which found that their decision-making priorities changed over the different phases of the buying cycle. What was important to them in the initial conversations with potential suppliers had a very different priority to what was important in a formal pitch situation. With this in mind, take any opportunity that you can to question the prospective client to find out, objectively, what is important to them in the pitch rather than work based on your own assumptions.

> Question the prospective client to find out, objectively, what is important to them in the pitch rather than work based on your own assumptions.

As part of your planning for these pitches and your role in them, the following are a selection of questions which might be helpful for you to consider, grouped together into some key areas.

Tapping into what has worked in the past

What can we learn from similar pitches that have been successful in the past?

You and your organisation have been involved in pitches before. What has worked? Identify the salient elements of past pitches that have been successful in relation to content, team dynamics and impact. Modelling what works is a hallmark of successful pitching.

Your audience

Every presentation needs to be audience centric. Even more so with pitches. We still work with some organisations that spend far too much time at the front end credentialising, rather than reflecting back what the prospective client wants and then identifying how to match their needs. Buyers are busy and inundated with information. You need to be able to connect the value of your solution to that specific buyer, or panel, otherwise the decision-makers are not going to give you any time or attention.

▌ What are the expectations of the audience?

▌ What can we do to identify what they want?

▌ Do we *know* what they want to see and hear from us (or are we assuming)?

▌ What do they think and feel about us now? How do we need them to feel about us at the end if we are to secure our outcome?

▌ What do we need to say to demonstrate that we understand them?

▌ How can we match their team with ours?

Outcomes

This may be obvious – however, it is good to get real clarity about the purpose of the meeting. Get really clear about the common outcomes.

▌ What is the specific objective/outcome for this meeting?

▌ How many stages are there in the decision-making process?

BATNA

A BATNA (developed by William Ury, Roger Fisher and Bruce Patton, the authors of *Getting to Yes: Negotiating Agreement Without Giving In*, a book on effective negotiation) is a 'Best Alternative to A Negotiated Agreement'. You may well be in a competitive tendering process. What will happen if you don't win? How much will you have to negotiate over price or other terms? You will typically be more confident and be able to negotiate more successfully if you have identified a BATNA, which is likely to be another opportunity for similar work with a different client.

▌ Do you have a BATNA?

▌ What can you do to improve your BATNA?

> ▌ You will typically be more confident and be able to negotiate more successfully if you have identified a BATNA.

Roles and responsibilities

If you are the most senior leader, there might be an expectation from the group that you will coordinate and chair the meeting. This may coincide with what you think will work best. There is a lot to be said for others to lead here and for you to play a dual role – add a key piece perhaps about strategy or vision and also go meta to the process and identify what works and does not work in relation to the process and the personnel involved in the pitch.

▌ Who is going to be the team leader? What are the other roles and responsibilities?

▌ If a member of your team chairs the meeting, then what role are you going to play?

▌ How many do you need on the team? Beware of having too many involved. Ideally match the number of people on the client side.

▌ Decide who should be responsible for answering which questions.

Engaging the audience with key messages

You want to avoid boring the audience. One of our clients, a facilities management company, creates storyboards to illustrate their offering, which is a great way to engage any audience and bring your pitches to life.

It is critical here that how you position your service is immediately identifiable to the audience and what they consider important. Canned elevator pitches just don't work. Your messaging needs to be succinct. Consider the Power of 3 here – what are the three key factors that will resonate the best?

▌ What are our differentiators?

▌ What are our core messages? What are our three key messages?

▌ What is the one thing that will make the biggest difference?

▌ How can we make our pitch memorable?

▌ What can we do to bring the pitch to life?

> It is critical here that how you position your service is immediately identifiable to the audience and what they consider important.

Preparing for questions and objections

Most pitches will combine a formal presentation and questions from the prospective client. Ideally, you want to restrict your pitch to the minimum amount of time because it is often the questions and discussion piece which will give your team the opportunity to shine. You are looking, ideally, for a collaborative discussion. It is highly likely that the prospective client will have some objections – these are hurdles that will potentially prevent them choosing you as the supplier. These need to be identified and thought through with a key person in the team allocated to handle the objection, should it arise.

▌ What questions have we been asked in similar pitches?

▌ What are our weaknesses?

▌ What are the five worst questions that we don't want to get asked and how would we answer them?

▌ You may or may not be the frontrunner. If you were in their shoes, what would stop you being awarded the work? What are the likely objections?

Priorities and practical tips

Pitching for work can be expensive, time-consuming and tough because your service or product may be rejected. Many of us will have been subjected to boring or feature-heavy sales presentations. They key is to engage the audience – bored buyers do not buy! You'll need to find ways to hook the audience, look like a team and be memorable. So here are some very practical ideas that will help you in your preparation and decision-making.

▌ Identify the procurement/decision-making process. It is easy to make assumptions about the decision-making process. Ensure you get definitive information about this.

▌ Give yourself enough time for the whole process. We are often brought into work with pitch teams and so often they feel under pressure because they have miscalculated the amount of time it takes to get a great pitch off the ground. While there will be pitches when the timescales are tight, you need to start the planning process as early as possible.

▌ Lobby in advance to build rapport. Sometimes the procurement process limits your ability to ask questions about the pitch. This is because the organisation wants to be as objective as possible and ensure there is a level playing field. Wherever possible find ways of meeting with or speaking to individuals to identify in more detail what the client wants. Rapport is still a critical element in the decision-making process and the more you can build this before the formal pitch the better. We worked with an organisation in which they lost a pitch, but then won it when the panel reviewed and decided that in fact they liked them more, even though objectively they were second best.

▌ Identify your best team. As you are planning your presentation, make sure you keep everyone in the loop in terms of amendments so that you create a 'no surprise' culture.

▌ Think carefully about the constituency of the team. Numbers wise your team should match theirs. Identify who you will be presenting to and then match around gender, expertise and ability to present well.

▌ If there is a large team, not everyone needs to contribute to the presentation but signpost this to the client.

▌ Sometimes you may have to field a large team. Avoid the mistake of thinking everyone has to present. You may have some in the team who only contribute in the discussion after the pitch. It can appear odd and confusing if too many in the team present. You may have a technical expert there to field specific questions.

▌ Meet as a pitch team before pitching. One of our core messages in this book is practice will get you closer to perfect. A formal pitch requires detailed planning and rehearsing is a critical phase. Most suppliers look the same technically so it's how you come across as a team that counts. This is not the time to sit on your feelings. As a leader you can play a key part in encouraging open and honest feedback during rehearsal. Accept feedback yourself as appropriate. Remember that the pitch starts the moment your team enters the room so even that needs practice. Agree simple and elegant handovers between presenters that appear seamless. Equally during the actual presentation, support each other with positive body language – good eye contact, nodding and complete focus on the delivery.

▌ Develop a strong opening statement. People remember the first things they are told. So have a memorable spike that gets to the heart of what the client wants, or the problem that you can solve with your service. Avoid the waffly or nervous preamble that is part of far too many pitches.

▌ Can you develop a STAR: 'Something They'll Always Remember'? There may well be several parties pitching. How will you stand out? Think of a STAR which may be a USP (Unique Selling Proposition) or key differentiator and repeat it several times during your presentation.

▌ Show your enthusiasm for winning the work/sale. Buyers will be engaged by people who are keen for the work. Remember that being enthusiastic is not the same as appearing 'needy'!

▌ Agree how you will manage questions.

▌ Decide the process as part of your planning. It is best for one individual to field questions and identify who is ideally suited to answer the questions you think will be asked.

▌ Be prepared for what to do if time is cut short in the pitch.

▌ Although potentially unfair, you may face a situation in which you have less time to pitch. Decide what to do if you have less time and how you would reshape your presentation, focusing on the core messages.

▌ Review and follow up immediately afterwards, and get feedback.

▌ Review as a team as soon as is possible. Ask yourself:

  ▌ What worked?

  ▌ What was the reaction of the audience?

  ▌ What would we do differently if we could pitch again?

  ▌ What have we learned that will improve future presentations?

Ensure you get feedback from one of the decision-makers as soon as possible, although practically this is likely to be after the decision has been made. Even if you don't win, you can use the feedback to make your written and verbal pitch even stronger for the future. Get them to be as specific as possible and avoid shying away from criticism.

17

How to deliver difficult or challenging messages

resenting difficult or challenging messages in a group
environment requires you to plan even more carefully
than usual to ensure that your message is heard in the
way you want it to be. When emotions are high it is easy for
your audience to read things into your words and make their
own interpretations of your message.

Examples of difficult messages or conversations might include:

▌ introducing new working procedures;

▌ selling a change in strategy that might have a negative
impact on your audience;

▌ announcing and discussing business results that are not as
good as were predicted;

▌ announcing new business/departmental targets or goals.

> When emotions are high it is easy for
> your audience to read things into your
> words and make their own
> interpretations of your message.

When presenting difficult or challenging messages you need
to recognise that there are likely to be emotional

undercurrents and offline conversations. This might extend into a difference between what an audience says and what it feels about the message. You cannot change that but you can plan to ensure that your message is not misinterpreted.

Questions to ask yourself

As part of your planning for these presentations, the following are a selection of questions which might be helpful for you to consider.

▌ What is my message?

Focus on defining a clear and succinct message and this will help guide your content and structure.

▌ What is my goal?

Be specific and challenge yourself to ensure that it is realistic based on:

a. how the audience are likely to be feeling about your message;

b. the amount of time you have to present; and

c. how you need or want your audience to feel at the end of your presentation.

▌ What can I do to lobby in advance?

Can you speak to individuals in advance to check their views and specific concerns and ensure that your presentation takes account of these? This enables you to better pace the group at the start of your presentation and helps remove the guesswork around how the audience might react to your message.

▌ Put yourself in the audience's shoes – what questions might they have that need addressing?

Possibly in conjunction with lobbying in advance, consider the specific questions that the audience may have in their mind based on the topic on which you are presenting. This will further inform your content to ensure that you provide clear answers where you can.

▌ What's in it for them?

Pay particular attention to identifying what would be helpful from the audience's perspective in terms of giving benefits (or avoidance of negative consequences) that they can relate to and see benefit in.

▌ How, realistically, do you want them to feel at the end of the presentation?

Think about their likely views/feelings about the topic at the start of your presentation and how long you have with them during the presentation. What would be a realistic shift for you to achieve in the time available?

▌ What action do you want them to take at the end of the presentation?

Be clear and specific about what you want: what are your desired actions for the audience at the end of the presentation?

▌ What style of approach should I use here? Be conscious of it.

Consider how you want to come across (e.g. supportive, understanding, authoritative, empathic, directive, etc.) to your audience and how to best achieve this during your presentation.

▌ How will I deal with negative reaction during the presentation?

What reactions might I get before, during or after the presentation? How will I handle these reactions if they occur? How will I manage the audience's expectations around how any concerns or reactions will be managed? What can I do in advance of the presentation to be as prepared as possible to manage reactions?

▎ What support do I have within the community I am
   addressing?

   Have I lobbied the audience (or a selection of the audience)
   in advance so that I better understand their views, concerns
   and thoughts? Who do I have support from? Can I leverage
   support from certain influential individuals to help
   influence others?

Priorities and practical tips

By their very nature these presentations are unlikely to
be enjoyable for you. When planning and delivering a
presentation that contains challenging or difficult messages
there are a few practical things you can pay attention to
in order to increase the chance of achieving a successful
outcome.

▎ Pace the audience

   Depending on the message, and the knowledge that the
   audience has about what is to come, it is possible that
   emotions will surface and so it is critical to demonstrate
   empathy with the group from the start. Consider their
   perspective and how they might be feeling and include some
   pacing statements (see Chapter 6 for more details) at the start
   of your presentation. Remember that pacing is designed to
   acknowledge how the audience *might* feel rather than telling
   them what they *do* feel at the start of your presentation. It is
   important that they feel that you understand their situation
   before they will be prepared to fully engage with your
   message and the rest of the presentation. Create three or four
   statements that acknowledge the feelings and views there
   might be in the room.

▎ Identify how *you* feel about this situation and message

   When you have to deliver a difficult or challenging
   message it helps for you to get very clear on specifically

how you think and feel about it. Without taking time to do this you run the risk of giving unclear messaging to your audience and sending out body language that may be at odds with the words you say. Having a clear understanding will aid clear preparation and delivery.

▌ Practise delivering your key message – beware the 'pillow effect'

When we deliver the key message we need to deliver it clearly and unambiguously. The discomfort we might feel about communicating the message can lead us to fall foul of the 'pillow' effect: we wrap the message up in unnecessary language with the intention of softening how it is heard and, in doing so, create uncertainty and possibly ambiguity in the audience. Practise delivering the message to ensure that you avoid the 'pillow effect'.

▌ Rehearse and get feedback from other senior people

If the message is important, it's important enough to rehearse. Make the time to have at least one complete run through from beginning to end and, ideally, seek to get feedback on how you deliver from other senior people in the business.

▌ Be clear on what action you want the audience to take as a direct result of the presentation

Consider the specific actions you want the audience to commit to if any. If not a specific action, consider what you want them to know or understand as a result of your presentation.

▌ Frame your messaging to ensure your message is not misinterpreted

There is a concept called the Fundamental Attribution Error that can easily lead to our messages, especially in difficult or challenging situations, being misinterpreted by our audience. When we make a statement the audience will hear what we say but will also unconsciously decide our motivation and intention in making the statement. While we can easily control what we say we cannot control how someone interprets meaning from it but we can take steps to positively influence them.

Framing is a technique that works on the basis that we clearly articulate our intention *before* we make the statement. This heads off the natural tendency for the listener to make their own interpretation of our intent and often enables the message to be heard more clearly.

Example: Assume that you have to present some feedback to a sales team from a client where there are a few things that need to be changed. As you think about how the sales team will hear this message you are aware that some might feel it is criticism of them personally and that you may not appreciate the difficulties they experience in their daily management of the expectations of this particularly demanding but important client. The message you want to give relates to some new standards of client care that you need to implement. Framing this message might involve first confirming that we have a client who is both demanding in their expectations and very important to the company. You might further state that you are aware of some of the challenges that have been experienced in managing expectations and that a lot of the sales team have worked long and hard to meet service standards. You might finish the framing by reinforcing that you have complete faith in the intention, standards and work ethic of the sales team and that what you need to discuss relates to some small changes. Now when you make your key point about implementing some changes the audience will be far less likely to be second guessing what your intention is.

▌ Operate within your Circle of Influence and have your audience do the same

One thing that is helpful to pay attention to, both for yourself as presenter and for your audience, is the need to focus your time and attention on only those things over which you can exert some influence or control. It is too easy sometimes, especially when we are focusing on something difficult or challenging, to concern ourselves with a number of things, including some over which we have no control or influence. This has the impact of making us feel less in control and, potentially, more negative. Your presentation should focus on those aspects that you and the audience can change and influence.

18
Setting a new vision/strategy

As a leader, you may be responsible for defining and/or communicating a vision or strategy for the company, department or your own team. You may be presenting to your own team or to a public audience or possibly to a board or executive team. Presentations around strategy or vision often require you to engage an audience so that they connect with a desired future outcome, a way of doing things or a change in some aspect of how they work. While you may be clear on the reasons and benefits of the strategy or vision, your audience may not be and your presentations in this context are likely to be part of a much bigger piece of work – so you definitely need to focus on preparation.

> While you may be clear on the reasons
> and benefits of the strategy or vision,
> your audience may not be.

Presentations around strategy and vision might be impacted by:

▊ people being uncertain about change and having a fear of the unknown;

▊ internal politics: people may not always say what they think or feel; and

▌ different views on the strategy or vision that might exist within your audience.

Presenting around topics relating to strategy and vision is often linked with leading change and, as a big part of leading change is about engaging an audience emotionally, you are likely to need to pay particular attention to emotions and possible concerns.

Questions to ask yourself

As part of your planning for these presentations, the following are a selection of questions which might be helpful for you to consider.

▌ How does this audience *feel* about the proposed strategy/ vision?

Can you take a sample of views in advance of preparing your presentation to better understand (rather than assume) how your audience feels about the proposed strategy or vision? Are they positively disposed, agnostic or perhaps feeling unsure or unhappy with the idea? If it is not practical to sample views then put yourself in their shoes and be as objective as possible in predicting how they might be feeling. Identifying how the audience feels will help you plan how best to engage them with your message.

▌ What do they need to know in order to engage with your strategy and message?

What information will your audience need in order for them to really buy into the strategy or vision that you are presenting? Rather than planning your presentation from a purely information-giving standpoint, consider what they might need in light of the question above. Perhaps they need reassurance or a sense of what this means for them as individuals or why this is so important. Remember that people buy emotionally and then justify logically, so ensure you appeal to the emotion and not just deliver a fact-loaded presentation.

❚ What is the burning platform and how can I best communicate this in a compelling way?

A key element of gaining buy-in to something new is identifying the personal 'What's In It For Me?' (WIIFM) for the proposed new vision or strategy for the audience members. Identify what the positive benefits of this proposed strategy or vision are and the negative consequences of not proceeding and help individuals see this in as personal terms as possible. Rather than seeking to create fear you are looking to connect individuals with why engaging with the new vision or strategy is important, relevant and beneficial for them.

❚ What is the best way to communicate this information?

There are a number of options available to you in terms of how you can present information so you might want to consider an alternative to the formal presentation. Depending on the size of your audience, whether they are in one location or geographically distributed, whether you want to create a more informal atmosphere or perhaps something more creative you could choose from a number of alternatives to a formal, slide-driven presentation. As strategy and vision connect with emotion you should consider the best and most appropriate means of supporting this imperative.

❚ What sort of take-away does the audience need?

What do you need your audience to be able to understand and recall after your presentation has finished? Consider providing a summary of the key points as a take-away or perhaps something symbolic and memorable that can act as a reminder of a key message or metaphor that you use. This might be an image, an object for the desk or something else that connects with your vision or strategy.

▌ To what extent has my senior team bought into this/ understand their role/are prepared to role model?

If you are presenting as the leader of a senior team, the impact and effectiveness of your presentation can be either supported or undermined by the views and behaviours of your team members. When considering your presentation it is helpful to identify the extent to which your senior team has bought into the new vision and strategy and the extent to which they understand their role in supporting what you are trying to achieve. Your presentation is only one aspect of communicating and implementing a successful strategy.

Critical in successful implementation of strategy is the notion that your senior team prioritise the needs of the business over the needs of their individual departments. Patrick Lencioni in his book *The Five Dysfunctions of a Team* suggests that it is often the case that members of the senior team prioritise the needs of their own department over those of the business. While this might be natural, it can be damaging especially when you are looking to implement a new or changed strategy.

Your senior team must support your strategy both in front of the audience to whom you are presenting and when they get back to their office and are working with their own department. Working with your team in advance of any presentation and addressing any interferences, specifically looking at the importance of role modelling the behaviours and support necessary for success, is critical in situations where the change you are seeking to bring about requires the proactive support of your immediate team.

▌ How, realistically, do I want my audience to feel at the end of the presentation?

Considering how you want your audience to feel after your presentation will help guide and inform both your content and your approach. Emotion is important if action is to be taken after your presentation, so think about how, specifically, you would like or need the audience to feel if they are to commit in the way you want them to with the strategy or vision. Thinking about this might inform whether your presentation can achieve this on its own or whether it needs to be part of a bigger process of communication and engagement as is often the case. Pay attention to how long you have for the presentation, how your audience is likely to feel at the start of your presentation about this topic and use this to be realistic about what is possible in the time available.

▌ What, specifically, is my outcome?

Be specific about what success for the presentation will look like. What do you want your audience to commit to, understand or be able to do as a result of your presentation? Is your presentation simply about informing them or is it about engaging them in change? If it is about change, what do you want to see happen as a result of the presentation and is this realistic to expect?

Priorities and practical tips

There is often a lot riding on presentations around strategy and vision. It might be that your presentation is the first communication that your audience will have about a topic that will be important to them and to how they see their role so it is important to plan effectively to maximise your success.

▌ Start with a compelling burning platform or spike

One thing that people need in order to engage fully with any substantial change is a 'burning platform', or compelling reason, for the change. Without it, there is a chance that individuals will not see change as a priority. With any presentation on strategy or vision you are often seeking to change minds and you need to give a clear and compelling reason for the change that individuals can really associate with and understand.

As part of this it might help to consider, and then articulate towards the start of your presentation, the positive consequences of change and the negative consequences of not changing. Take the time to personalise this to your audience so that they can see the importance to them.

▌ Credentialise the strategy/vision – social influence

Linked with the point above, consider how you can credentialise the strategy or vision that you are presenting. What external trends, research or statistics can you use to make your proposed strategy even more credible? People tend to follow people who are seen as credible, knowledgeable experts so what can you do to leverage this? When uncertain, people also tend to look to the actions and behaviours of others to determine their own. Can you leverage this concept of social influence to build greater buy-in?

▌ Pace the audience – acknowledge their possible feelings/ experiences

At the start of your presentation, especially if your audience might have some concern about the proposed strategy or vision, ensure that you spend enough time pacing them. This demonstrates empathy by putting yourself in their shoes and recognising what feelings and views might be present in the audience. It is important that the audience feels that you understand what they might be feeling before you earn the right to lead them forward towards your proposed strategy or vision. Trying to lead them too quickly runs the risk of not gaining the buy-in necessary for your presentation to be effective.

▌ Finish with a powerful final message

People remember the first thing you say and the last thing so ensure that you create a powerful final message that supports your 'call to action' (what it is that you want them to do as a result of the presentation). A strong final message can either connect with the burning platform for this change, summarise the key points you wanted to make in a clear and compelling way, or link to a metaphor that your audience can relate to easily.

▌ Ensure your body language supports your conviction in the message

Ensure that you proactively manage your state so that your body language conveys the conviction and confidence that you want to communicate. Your words need to be aligned with your body language so if you notice that you are lacking confidence or some other resource then pay attention to it and manage it proactively. Chapter 12 in this book on confidence will provide useful tips on how to do this.

▌ Involve your audience if possible

Engagement can be supported by encouraging your audience to participate and contribute. By posing questions and making a presentation more interactive you can build individual and group awareness and responsibility. If a group is encouraged to think about the topic rather than just listen to information being given to them they are more likely to buy into it. Plan your presentation to include, where appropriate, some questions to provoke thought and discussion.

▌ Test with senior team

With the buy-in, support and active participation of your senior team often being crucial to long-term success it would help to test your approach and presentation with them. Elicit the views of your team on what needs to be covered and the best way of achieving it where appropriate and possible. Rehearse the presentation with the team and elicit their specific feedback, including on what works well and what suggestions they have for change.

▌ Create a one-page document that summarises vision pictorially

It is often helpful to create a simple one-pager that uses a metaphor or graphic to provide an aide memoire of the key points of your strategy presentation and which links to the key themes.

19

Presenting in the boardroom

Depending on your current role you may have to present in the boardroom, either as the chair or as a senior leader. For the purposes of this chapter we are assuming you have to present to the board – directors, senior executives or stakeholders. Here is your moment to 'shine and share' your research, ideas, project updates or even financial performance. These kinds of presentation are often intimate because you are presenting to a small group and they can support or detract from your personal credibility. They can potentially be nerve-wracking if you are not part of the board, and will be pivotal to the acceptance of an idea or getting the green light for your part of the organisation. Think of the analogy of presenting in the *Dragons' Den* TV programme: it's a 'make or break' situation where the stakes are high. Your ability to demonstrate that you have prepared effectively and have the necessary background information in case you are grilled for more detail on a particular topic is critical. You, and maybe also your team, have worked hard to bring this information to the table. So it is imperative that the presentation is imparted with professionalism and enthusiasm that will have those gathered around the table keen to learn more ... and not doze off or become confused by what you are saying.

Questions to ask yourself

▌ What support do I have on the board already?

▌ What allies can I rely on?

▌ How do they view me and my credibility? Do I have sufficient support for my ideas?

▌ How will they feel about me and the content/topic?

▌ What is my desired outcome and is it realistic?

▌ What concerns will they have and what questions will they ask?

▌ How can I be concise and still compelling?

▌ Who is/are key decision-makers, and how are decisions made?

▌ What do they need to read or know in advance of the presentation?

Priorities and practical tips

So what are the key ideas for how to present in the boardroom with success? Here are some tips that will not only make your presentation a success in the boardroom, but spoken about in the 'hallways'. Think of the 3 Ps – preparation, practice and passion.

▌ Lobby in advance

What can you do to sow the seeds or start the persuasion process before the presentation? Is there a template the board likes to work from? What past presentations have worked well? Do you know team members who have a good reputation for making effective board presentations? If you do, get with some of them and identify how they do it. Rehearse your presentation with someone who can give you constructive feedback. Ask some of the key

board members what they need to know about the
subject. Test some of your ideas and get feedback. Who
can you count on for support? Do as much as you can to
lobby in advance, so that your presentation gets the
support required or you make the favourable impression
required.

▌ Know your topic

This is key to success – if you have not mastered your brief,
or there are huge holes in your knowledge of the subject
matter, it will have a direct impact on your ability to get
traction for your idea and reduce your gravitas and
standing with the head honchos. Get real clarity about the
information you are imparting. Make sure you ask the key
questions of your team, review your findings again to
ensure you have the required background information, and
have back-up data to hand that you may or may not use.
Find ways to link what you are presenting to core business
challenges or strategy so you are seen as someone who sees
the bigger picture.

▌ Be clear on your message

The board will want you to get to the point immediately.
Be clear about your purpose, outcomes and the benefits of
whatever you are proposing. Get clarity about what you
want to communicate and get to your key messages as soon
as possible. Have a list of the main points of the
presentation, to refer to, making sure you don't forget
something – this will stop you from rambling and going off
the subject.

▌ Bring the subject to life

Don't read the slides – they are there as a supporting
resource. It is your role to bring the data alive with real-life
scenarios, stories and case studies. There is nothing more
boring than someone standing reading stats from a slide.
Don't be that person. If you need to show a product or a

design, then have them with you, taking enough for everyone who will be at the presentation.

▍Positive thinking

For many people, access to the boardroom is like being invited into a secret society. There is certainly a mystique about it in some people's eyes. Your beliefs about your worth and being accepted may be influencing your feelings of intimidation or sense of welcome ease. So your mental preparation for your presentation should actually start days before. Use some of the techniques around confidence identified in Chapter 12. Picture yourself delivering with confidence, use diaphragmatic breathing and anything else that works to get you in the zone.

▍Arrive early

If possible go to the boardroom before the meeting and make sure that the equipment is set up and everything is working. Have your bag there with all your resources and handouts within easy reach. You don't want to be fumbling for things with everyone waiting for you.

▍Develop your resilience

Presenting in the boardroom can be one of the most intimidating of places to speak. You may well be grilled and be asked some tough questions. You should expect tough questions, prepare for them and fight your corner. You need to demonstrate resilience.

▍Body language

Dress in something that makes you feel good about yourself and powerful. When you enter the room, remember to breathe, walk tall and be confident. Take your seat and as the time comes closer for you to present, stand straight up and walk to the front of the table with your head held high – not unfolding yourself out of the chair and stumbling to the front as you knock into the backs of chairs and fumble with papers.

Part

Your path to presenting success

Following up to get the result you want

We were working with a top business leader recently on a keynote presentation that was to be delivered at their annual conference. He had many of the attributes of a great presenter – a strong knowledge base, a high level of confidence, charisma and a great voice. We worked with him on brainstorming the key messages and structuring a coherent argument, and he understood the importance of rehearsing his content and fine-tuning his delivery. With a month or so to go he was in a good place. Then we asked him – how was he going to ensure his ideas for the new direction had traction back in the workplace? How was he going to get feedback on this major strategic presentation? His face said it all – our questions were met with a blank stare. He had not thought these through.

Many leaders pay little or no attention to the follow-up process. So many business presentations delivered by leaders are focused on 'the event' itself and, in too many instances, that is the end of the matter. This chapter focuses on two elements. First, specific ideas that will help create the conditions for strategically important presentations to achieve the necessary leverage to encourage change or allow ideas to percolate throughout an organisation. And, second, how to get the feedback required so that a leader can improve his or her presentation capability.

Follow-up options

Presentations rarely deliver the result you want in isolation as a leader. Of course there are some presentations you will make as a leader/presenter in which you may not need to follow up – for example when you are presenting on past performance. However, many presentations require individuals, groups and teams to act. So if you have a presentation, for example, on new priorities, a change in strategy, a product or service launch, rebranding or new regulations affecting the business, you will want the core messages cascaded through the business. While the initial presentation will be critical in setting the right tone, following up is critical. It's so easy to not pay attention to this element. Everyone is busy and there will be many other priorities. So how do you create the conditions for your ideas to be understood, for people to act and individuals to change?

The first consideration is your outcomes. What are your goals in giving the presentation? What, ideally, do you want your people to do as a result of the presentation? Get clear on the changes in behaviour required, on what you want to see and when. You'll be comfortable with the SMART mnemonic:

> What **specifically** do you want?
>
> How will you be able to **measure** any changes?
>
> Be **ambitious** in what you want to happen.
>
> Be **realistic** – so what are the first steps?

And, finally, have a **timeframe** – when do you expect to notice improvements, changes and results?

Example

Imagine, as a leader, you were delivering a presentation on improving your internal communications. In addition to any strategic objectives, a SMART goal for your presentation may be:

At the end of the hour's presentation, colleagues will buy into the reasons for the new and improved structure of internal communications, their role in disseminating the information to their teams, and how to run a kick-off meeting to communicate the key messages, within the next month.

Once goals are agreed, it is time to decide a number of mechanisms to help spread the word and meet your outcomes. If we do not set up the conditions for action, change or learning transfer to take place after any presentation, the impact of the event itself and any learning that has happened because of the event will, in many cases, be lost. Everyone in business has heard of employee engagement. Most organisations will work at ensuring that their staff are fully involved emotionally and intellectually and perform enthusiastically at work. It hardly requires an MBA to recognise that engaged employees leads inexorably to better results, improved retention, an increase in customer satisfaction, higher productivity, and so on.

Many companies today think that email and mobile phone communications can solve all of their communications problems, but they can't. We need to find ways to embed the key messages for everyone so that, in turn, the organisation reaps the benefits of improved results. Communication helps individuals and groups coordinate activities to achieve goals, and it's vital in socialisation, decision-making, problem-solving and change-management processes. Internal communication is the basis for individuals and groups to make sense of their organisation, what it is and what it means.

> Internal communication is the basis for individuals and groups to make sense of their organisation, what it is and what it means.

An effective follow-up communication plan to a strategically important presentation:

- ensures consistent delivery of information;
- creates a sense of belonging – well-informed employees feel more involved and have an increased sense of ownership;
- enables an organisation to operate more consistently;
- helps reduce conflict;
- helps establish priorities;
- helps enable change;
- reinforces desired behaviours within the organisation;
- eliminates silo mentality;
- enables more effective decision-making;
- ensures efficient use of limited resources;
- helps build relationships across organisational boundaries.

Effective communications can be achieved through external consultants, or internally via senior managers, the HR or L&D functions and internal channels.

Before deciding which mechanisms will work best, consider the following list of questions, which will help guide you as to what will work most efficiently:

▌ How is your presentation likely to be received?

▌ What level of buy-in or conflict are you likely to face?

▌ What additional information needs to be cascaded?

▌ Who are the key influencers that you need to get onside?

▌ How are they most likely to be influenced?

▌ How much budget do you have for the follow-up?

▌ Who needs to deliver the communication?

▌ What is the required frequency?

▌ What factors will impact the success or failure of the initiative (people, culture, interdependencies, time, budget, tools, etc.)?

▌ What do you want people to do as a result of your initial presentation?

▌ What supporting communications are needed to reinforce the message?

▌ What feedback mechanisms do you prefer?

▌ How will you measure the communications effectiveness?

▌ How will you respond to feedback?

▌ What are the real interferences that will hinder achievement of your desired outcomes?

Below is a range of mechanisms that we have seen work.

Mechanism	Ideas	Benefits
Send out video of presentation	Could be full video or edited highlights Capture feedback on day from attendees and add in introduction from you as presenter or endorsement from business sponsor Accompany the video with your slideshow	Key messages coming directly from you Quick and easy to produce
Follow-up webinar or face-to-face Q&A	Questions can be taken immediately If there is a follow-on Q&A then collect questions at the time of the presentation Do a number of face-to-face or webinar Q&As Send constant reminders Record and send out using appropriate channel	People can hear directly from you Real concerns or issues can be raised and handled Easy to set up and broadcast
Create a one-pager outlining idea	Concentrate on the key messages – if possible use the Power of 3 Could use an infographic Can be used with a variety of channels – noticeboards, intranet, sent by email, included in newsletter	Distils into manageable chunks for people – ease of communication and good for 'big picture' people Really gets you to think about core messages Increases likelihood of everyone being on the same page!

Mechanism	Ideas	Benefits
Write thought leadership paper	Allows greater detail to be introduced	Good for those who like detail
	Think about co-authoring with other interested parties	Can lay out strategic thinking
	Could be used externally on social media, etc.	Gets you to really think through whole initiative
Team briefings	Schedule briefings soon after initial presentation	Ensures that staff at all levels receive information that is relevant to them
	Train managers/presenters and develop a template so you get consistency in communications	Provides a consistent and measurable process for conveying strategic and operational information
	Attend a few and answer questions	Gets you feedback in a safe environment
		Gets buy-in up and down the organisation
		Teams can set their own action plans
Workshops	Use if you want action and movement as a direct result of your presentation	If you are looking for action workshops can be better than a team briefing
	Creates conditions for empowerment	Can be targeted at right level in organisation
	Identify specific outcomes	
	Ensure workshop leaders are competent facilitators	
	Provide pre-reading beforehand which will help acceleration to action	
	Ensure actions are visible and people held to account	

In addition to these specifics, think about the use of other passive or interactive channels of communication that you can use to engage people in follow-up.

Passive channels

To get your message spread far and wide you must acknowledge that employees will pick up information from many different channels:

▌ intranet

▌ Wiki

▌ notice boards

▌ posters

▌ email

▌ print.

Interactive channels

Face-to-face interaction will work best so pick the types that are relevant to your presentation:

▌ company conference

▌ business unit briefing

▌ inductions

▌ breakfast briefings

▌ director back to the shop floor

▌ lunchtime learning

▌ blogs

▌ discussion forums

▌ instant messaging and social media.

Getting the right feedback

The second element of following up presentations is the leader's ability to identify ways to improve as a presenter. Being a leader can be lonely. It can be really tough to get sensible feedback on your management style and how you lead. The same applies for presentations. Picture the scene – a leader completes a presentation and comes off the stage pumped up and pleased with how it went. In the break afterwards he is surrounded by direct reports and other employees. He asks – how do you think my presentation went? The typical responses may well include 'really good', 'hit the mark', 'landed well with the audience', 'very effective'. The leader can easily be bamboozled into believing his own hype or the positivity and the generalised feedback of others who are reluctant to express their real views because of hierarchy, embarrassment, politeness or politics.

> It can be really tough to get sensible feedback on your management style and how you lead.

The most effective way to improve as a presenter is a combination of self-reflection and feedback from a trusted source. Self-reflection first. To avoid falling into the trap of believing your own hype, take some time to reflect on your presentation. The easiest way is to get the presentation recorded and play it back. Get really objective about this – most people are very critical about themselves and whenever we are giving feedback as trainers we have to bring presenters up on immediately focusing on the negative. So you are looking for balance here. When you spend time on the re-run use the following template:

Questions	Observations
How did the start go? Did you get to the heart of your presentation using a spike?	
What did you notice about your body language? Did you look confident, smile and get eye contact with as many of the audience as possible? Did your gestures support what you were saying?	
How was your voice? Was there variety and did you use both the credible and connector voice patterns?	
To what extent did your key messages land?	
Did the structure make sense to you as you review the presentation?	
How did you answer questions? Were your answers succinct and did you check with your questioners that they got a satisfactory answer?	
What, if any, cues can you pick up from the audience's reaction to your presentation?	
What worked really well?	
If you had the chance to present again, what changes would you make?	
What are your key learning points that you can take into the next presentation?	

The most beneficial way you can improve your future presentations is to use a trusted source – this could be a member of your own team or an external presentation coach (we are here to be hired! Visit www.theleadersguidetopresenting.com for contact details). For this to work, the trusted individual needs either to see the presentation or watch the video. Either way, think carefully about what sort of feedback you want, and avoid being defensive if you get feedback with which you disagree. Use the template above or a version of it and get the feedback as soon as possible after you have completed the presentation.

SUMMARY

▌ Get clear about the goals for follow-up.

▌ Brainstorm and then prioritise internal communications mechanisms that will work most effectively.

▌ Identify successes for future presentations.

▌ Feedback is the breakfast of champions.

▌ Spend time on self-reflection.

▌ Use a trusted advisor to help you recognise what is working and what you can do to improve future presentations.

▌ Use a feedback template to capture results.

Developing your capability

n line with our strong message that it is practice that develops a skill most quickly, we want to encourage you to both reflect on your own existing performance and plan tangible ways to develop and enhance your skills in this important area as a leader.

With this in mind we have created three elements of an action-oriented plan that can form the basis for your continued development as an outstanding presenter: taking stock, taking action and taking your time.

Taking stock is about self-reflection—considering how you are performing now in the key areas of presenting. Taking action is about what you can do through your actions in future presentations to increase their impact and effectiveness. Finally, taking your time provides a specific checklist for you to consider in advance of any future presentation to ensure you have considered the important aspects and questions for you to consider in your planning phase, a phase that it is critical you make enough time for.

Taking stock

Elements of presenting	What am I doing currently?	What will I do differently?
1. Planning 2. Structuring presentations (including impactful start and finish) 3. Rehearsing 4. Getting into the right state 5. Managing my body language 6. Engaging the audience 7. Utilising my voice proactively 8. Answering questions 9. Seeking feedback from others		

Based on taking stock of the specific presentation elements listed above, you can now focus on identifying the key areas of strength and development for yourself. Complete these in the table below and be as specific as you can. It is easier to leverage strengths and improve development areas if you are really specific about them.

What are my key strength areas around preparing for and delivering presentations?	
What are my key development areas around preparing for and delivering presentations?	

Taking action

Task	My commitment	Resources required
My presentation goal: Make it SMART - e.g. make 15 presentations to a variety of audiences over the next 12 months and have received positive feedback from at least 3 sources		
Opportunities to present: What additional opportunities can I create to present more over the next 3–6 months in a variety of contexts?		
Knowledge and competence: What resources will I read/ review in order to develop my knowledge and competence in presenting?		
Improving audience engagement through my presentation style: Measures might include getting audience feedback, thinking about new and more creative ways to structure your presentations, etc.		
Develop the right habits: Use the checklist below and the results of your P-IQ (see www. theleadersguidetopresenting. com) to identify the key areas to focus on across all aspects of your presenting		

Taking your time

When you are preparing for or reflecting on a presentation it is often helpful to run through a checklist. Pilots do this at various stages before, during and after a flight and it helps ensure that they pay attention to all of the important things and do not forget critical tasks and checks. The checklist below provides a simple self-reflection tool to ensure that you are paying attention to the right things when you are planning for a high-stakes presentation.

> When you are preparing for or reflecting on a presentation it is often helpful to run through a checklist.

Presentation-specific question	My notes
Do I have a specific outcome for this presentation?	
Is my goal realistic given the time available and my understanding of the audience?	
What is the make-up of the audience?	
What can I do to lobby in advance?	
What do they feel about this topic and about me?	
What do they know about this topic and what do I need them to know?	
What is my confidence level as I think about this presentation to this audience and what do I need to do to ensure I am in the right state at the start?	
How do I want them to feel at the end of the presentation?	

▶

Presentation-specific question	My notes
What, specifically, do I want the audience to do as a result of this presentation?	
What are my core messages and can I distil them into three key points?	
When structuring my content for these core messages, does it fit within the $7^+/^-2$ rule?	
Have I created a compelling start (that includes a spike) and a compelling finish/ call to action?	
How, specifically, will I engage the audience during the presentation (e.g. have I created opportunities for discussion and interaction, used stories or metaphors, etc.)?	
What visual aids will captivate the audience and enhance my presentation?	
What creative methods other than PowerPoint can I use to present my message in a compelling way (e.g. story boards, video clips, etc.)?	
What handouts or additional resources (if any) do I need to create to support my presentation?	
What are the five worst questions I might be asked and have I prepared succinct, relevant and effective answers?	
Have I rehearsed and have I taken the opportunity to obtain objective feedback?	
How will I follow up this presentation to ensure I achieve my desired outcome?	

Summary

When we train leaders in presenting we always suggest that they keep the summary short and compelling and so we want to follow that model here.

We started this book by illustrating a four-layer model that incorporated all of the important elements of effective presenting and we show this again here.

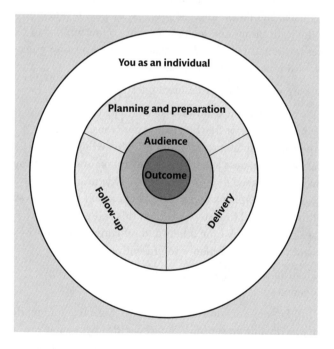

Throughout this book we have provided very practical 'how-tos' for each of these layers and believe that with this information you now have everything you need in order to present effectively as a leader.

As with many aspects of leadership, a theoretical knowledge of what you need to do will only take you so far. Skill is developed through action rather than simple understanding. It is too easy to fall into the trap of believing that you can 'think yourself into a new way of behaving' when actually you need to 'behave your way into a new way of thinking'. Pay attention to the ideas included in Chapter 21.

> Skill is developed through action rather than simple understanding.

Our experience in training leaders in presenting is that they can make significant and fast progress by paying attention to the right things and looking for more opportunities to present. What will, therefore, guarantee your success going forward now that you have read this book?

▌ Complete our P-IQ assessment questionnaire

We created a quick self-assessment diagnostic that you can fill in for free by visiting our website (www. theleadersguidetopresenting.com). This will give you greater awareness about where you are naturally strong and where you need to develop in terms of your presenting. No change happens without first having self-awareness so this is a useful first step. Build on this self-assessment by seeking feedback from others and reflecting yourself on your current performance in presenting.

▌ Have an action plan that is relevant to you and your context

Build a sense of what 'good progress' looks like for you in terms of your presenting. Being specific about what you are aiming for will help you recognise when you have achieved it.

▌ Practise on the edge of discomfort

Recognise that the only real way to develop and improve
a skill is to do more of it. There is no shortcut. Look
proactively for more opportunities to present in a variety of
situations. The more you present, the better you will get at
presenting!

▌ Take a continuous improvement approach to developing
your presenting skills

Use widely available resources such as TED and YouTube
to inform how you think and approach your own
presentations. Be curious about how others present and
what you can learn from every presentation that you see.

▌ Proactively seek to get good-quality feedback from people
you trust

How you *are* seen and perceived by others is more
important than how you *think* you are perceived.

Your own knowledge and expertise combined with the
information contained in this book on planning, structuring
and delivering presentations means that you now have
everything you need in order to be an outstanding presenter.
It is now up to you to put all of this into practice and make a
difference in your world.

What did you think of this book?

We're really keen to hear from you about this book,
so that we can make our publishing even better.

Please log on to the following website and leave
us your feedback.

It will only take a few minutes and your thoughts
are invaluable to us.

www.pearsoned.co.uk/bookfeedback

Index